THE WONDROUS CROSS

Best wishes Jeanette
Keep up the good work
love
Jane
x x

THE WONDROUS CROSS

(A GUIDE FOR THE SPIRITUAL PATHWAY)

BY

JANE S. McCARTHY

Printed by Cambrian Printers, Aberystwyth

FOREWORD

I dedicate this book to my long suffering husband, Chris,
who I adore.

Thank-you darling, for having so much patience with me.

Also, to all my unseen friends.

CONTENTS

CHAPTER ONE

The Beginning

One of the greatest paths in life is the spiritual path. True knowledge can only be found within oneself. By accepting yourself and understanding what you are and who you are, can lead to an inner knowledge that was there all the time.

You only have to ask. You only have to open the door when Christ knocks. In life, I have given many people the picture by Holman Hunt 'The Light of the World' and asked them to concentrate on the picture and say Yes Lord come in.

My life up until that time was one of a Christian. I cannot say I regularly attended church but I tried to lead a Christian life. My courtship with the church lead me to the Methodist way, in which I agreed that all churches are God's house and there is only one God. Today, I still think that the Methodist way is a good start for Christian living as each member is considered family. I was lucky in effect that our Minister was exceptional and I was volunteered to be in charge of the Anchor Boys, young Boys Brigade. That year was one of the happiest I had known as a member of a church. But the last four years have literally been the most amazing of my life and I have a story to tell. It is a story of a learning experience through the spiritual path which has lead to many weird and wonderful beginnings.

I was adopted and my parents would be considered by today's standard rather old to adopt. My mother and father were beautiful people and I was very lucky. My mother did not force religion on me but she was the more spiritual of my parents.

I remember my very first time in church, my Aunt Muriel lead me to the altar and the Minister placed his hand on my head. I must have been about four or five years old. I felt something and to this day I knew what I felt, but it has only been recently that I have understood.

My mother was very wise and taught me a strict Christian way and encouraged me to go to church and through daily life tried to teach me a way of life through love. I know it is not easy being a teenager for any generation but the patience she showed with love shone through. She was well loved in our community. The reason why I write of my mother is because it is relevant to my story later on.

I grew up and married and lived outside my home town. I still saw my parents regularly. I worked in a bank and lived a normal life. All the time I would have experiences, one could call deja vu; places I'd know although I had never been there; people I would meet, I'd know I had met them before. Strange dreams that came true. Always an inner voice helping and guiding.

One particular dream I had all through my teenage years. The dream progressed into a fantastic unbelievable story which I can remember still having well into my late twenties. At one stage, I started to write about the dream thinking it would probably make a good book.

Basically, it was about twins, one girl and boy. I dreamt that the girl was a Guardian and as she grew up, knowing she was different, visiting other worlds in a spaceship, which was controlled by her mind. The computer was 'on line' with her brain wave patterns. She only had to think the directions. As the dream progressed through the years, with many adventures on the way, a form of healing was apparent by using a white light from her hands. This white light was a form of energy which used on a dead planet, could slowly eradicate negativity and produce a healthy environment. She was called The Guardian as she protected the earth from outer space dangers. Her call sign was 'Snowbird.'

My mother had been ill for many years with angina and one day, whilst working in the bank, I received a phone call. My mother had been rushed to hospital with a heart attack. I remember rushing to the hospital by bus praying on the way. I asked My Lord, please let her hold her first grandson, something she always wanted. My mother recovered and did hold her first grandson - but that was years later. If only I knew then what I know now, I would have asked for her to hold her first grand daughter too - I never had a daughter.

One of the cross-roads of my life was the breakdown of my marriage, after the birth of my son. David was born on the 17 December 1981, he was actually due Christmas Day, but impatient then, as he is now, he decided to come early. After the birth, I went into terrible depression which lasted a long time. The crossroad was the very first months of being on my own with David and having to cope. I must admit these times were not pleasant but a true learning experience. The inner voice which helped and guided was now a reality, but had turned to mocking.

I have looked back on those experiences and realised it was the very beginning of mediumship.

My reality was now a different one. I have been asked to write it all down, but this is not an easy subject to write about. There were times when I heard voices and did not comprehend whether there was someone in the room, or not. I kept looking around for the place where the voice came from. When others in physical form were in the room, I could not distinguish whether they had said something, or was it one of the voices. I kept a lot to myself and I still do until now.

David was now around four years old. One day one of the voices said 'it is best you end it all.' I said no, I could not leave my son.

'Then take him with you.'

No. I could not do it. I was being bombarded by many voices at the same time. I realised they were trying to drive me to suicide.

The following day David, bless him, asked to go to nursery, so we went. That's when I decided to do something to help us. I stayed with my Mum and Dad for a fortnight. It was the best medicine anyone could have wished for. My mother never scolded, never criticised. I remember one night, I was cuddling David in bed, the voices never ceased, persecuting, mocking again. In my mind's eye I could see half a dozen people at the back of the garden through the bedroom window. Cuddling David closer, I was afraid. Not only was I hearing them, I was also seeing them. My mother came into the bedroom. I don't really know how she knew but she drew the curtains and placed a high back chair in front of the window. She then got into bed and cuddled me. I think it was the first night that I really slept for months. It was the start of the road to recovery.

The voices never went. When I was down, they got worse. When I was strong, they left me alone. I found I could cope as long as I could sleep in the night. My doctor prescribed sleeping tablets and my life started to take shape again. I went out and at the end of the year met Chris, my present long suffering husband, who I adore and luckily enough he adores us both.

My mother encouraged me to find a little part-time job and she would look after David. He was to start infants that year. Things were looking up. I found a job as an insurance clerk for a few hours a day. I started Monday and finished the same day.

My mother was dead.

My father found her on the kitchen floor, she was making an early cup of tea, something she had done for years early in the morning. My dad told me she had died with a smile on her face, she had looked so peaceful. She had only met Chris the once.

When one door closes, another one opens and in comes another angel sent by heaven.

Chris had only just lost his father when I met him and having been through his own personal grief, was able to be a rock of support through my terrible loss. It was all a blur, the preparation, the funeral, the family and then left to cope. My father was lost. Chris had lost both parents and he took a very rough ride with both my father and myself. For someone who I had only just met, he was at that time, my sole comforter and I might add still is.

David and I still lived on our own and I took him to our local church not long after the funeral. I find comfort in a church like nowhere else. We sang some hymns and then started prayers. We had sat at the back not being regulars to this church.

David suddenly stood up and shouted at the top of his voice.

'I hate you God, you took my Nan. Why did you take my Nan?'

People were turning and staring at us. David paid no attention and carried on having his conversation with his God, making his peace. He was only four years old. In the end, I took him out. The Minister of the Methodist church which I joined not long after this episode, bless him, was very wise and I cannot praise him enough. He told me it was a perfectly healthy reaction for a child, but never in one so young. David is very special.

My father went downhill. It had not seemed long before they had celebrated their 40th Wedding Anniversary. When you lose one parent you seem to cling to the last and I did just that. We went on holiday together with David and those memories I treasure. I was at a low ebb and the voices were coming through all the time. I was still taking sleeping tablets in the night to cope.

Although, when I imagined a picture of Christ, one of my favourite, the voices subsided and sleep took over. I used this method most nights and Christ gave me strength, knowing that he loved me - it helped.

I found that now I had some form of control, but I wished I could open that door to the other side and then close it.

I was extremely lucky, I have the best friends anybody could have wished for. Sheila, a night sister and Dave her husband helped and supported through those bad times. In the end, Dave made arrangements for me to see a professional medium.

I went with little or no thoughts of getting rid of the problem. We talked and Dave listened. I was told I was lucky. The last thing I wanted to hear. She told me I was not only claraudio; which basically means hearing spirits, clarvisual; the ability to see spirits but also psychic. I had guessed most of that through my life, but never did it effect me where there was no control. She told me that she had prayed for years to have the gifts that I wanted so much to get rid of. She lent me a book in which it explained a lot more about the subject and as the fear gradually left me, it was replaced by a deeper understanding of my faith in Christ. Now if the voices became too much, I prayed and through my faith, was able to gain some sort of control. I now know that this was one of the lower levels where more negative or dark forces can do their work.

Because of the years of having to cope with this problem, I closed the door for quite a few years. However, if a path in life is your path, it doesn't matter how many times you come off it, you will always be drawn back to do the work your spirit intended to do whilst here in this lifetime. This is exactly what happened to me. I was drawn to the Spiritualist church for the first time.

I sat in the pew not knowing exactly what happens. On the bus coming to church I said to myself, OK answer this question in church. The Minister was someone who was connected with my ex-husband's place of work and I vaguely recollected him. Prayers were said just like normal church, The Lord's Prayer and Prayers of healing. Then after a hymn is sung the Minister asks for those loved ones, in spirit, to come forward with messages for those of us left behind.

The Minister picked on me and not only stated -

'You asked a question on the way here and this is your answer.'

He told me I was at a crossroads in my life and that one day soon I would walk six feet tall.

I have always believed that when you die there was heaven and hell and depending upon your conduct, whilst living, you went to one or to the other. However, if spirits are with us, then they are still alive, but not living in our physical dimension. Spirits are our souls, the very essence of who we are and that part of who we are, is a part of God. Every living thing is part of God.

I married Chris that year in the Methodist church and I was honoured to have my favourite Minister marry us. I hold a picture dear to me, one of Chris and I on our wedding day with my father and my Minister standing by us. These three men have had the most influence on my life and I might add the only three men I have admired and looked up to.

Even on my wedding day the voices raged. They would not leave me alone even on that sacred occasion. I don't think there was one person in that celebration who knew the truth of my inner turmoil. I now know that the negative forces, the lower levels, did not wish me to marry Chris as he was to become the stabilising influence in my life, enabling me in the future, to complete my tasks in life - walking, living and working with God, in every moment of every day.

It become apparent when settling down to married life, I had to overcome what I had felt was an infliction. With help from Chris and my good friends, I stopped taking sleeping tablets. Life was fine and that Christmas was one of the happiest I had known. My father, who was living alone came to stay with us.

Dad now had a girlfriend who he went everywhere with and was starting to enjoy life again. He had taken a few trips abroad and was looking happy and relaxed. We all went for a meal Boxing Day and met up with further life long friends from Aberystwyth. What a celebration, a real family occasion, tinged with sadness as my mum wasn't around to enjoy it.

Dad left the next day, I had to go back to work. I was working full time in insurance. I started not long after Chris and I were married. Again, it was not easy to do, as in every stressful time in my life, at that stage, the voices relished the opportunity to persecute me. At times, when I first started due to the location of the typists, which were behind me, I didn't really know if it was them talking or my voices. Looking back on those times, I must admit, they must have thought me very aloof and not at all friendly.

But believe me, it is not easy hearing the things I do and not knowing who said them. It was easier for me to just carry on working hard, ignoring all voices, whether physical or otherwise. So at this stage in my book, I want to thank those colleagues who persevered with me and helped although not really understanding. How could they. It has only been the last years I have really talked about my experiences. So Bless those colleagues and I thank you. You never knew the truth, forgive me for not telling you.

After three months, I had settled in and I was quite happy to go back to work that morning following Boxing Day. Half way through the morning Chris appeared at my desk.

My father was dead.

It was sudden, a heart attack. Oh! how lost I was. The very thought of never seeing my father again. He was my mentor, my father and my dearest companion. I always took everything to him. It was like the sun had stopped shining. I had now lost both parents so quickly, within years of each other.

As you can now probably imagine, again a very stressful time and again the voices raged. Persecution. Wow! it was bad. How I survived that time I do not know. My two angels, Chris and David supported and helped. I took time from work but quickly realised with my mind unoccupied the voices raged worse. I returned and resumed as best I could. I never lost my faith and as I worked I became stronger and as I became stronger so did my faith. Christ was not only someone in the Bible, He was very real to me.

Summer came and with it a move to the family home in Rhiwbina. I had always come home in trouble and I felt at peace. But now strange occurrences were happening on a daily basis. I could pick up on people and knew what was going to happen to them. I started to do the cards, that is, by using ordinary playing cards was able to read people's future. It was uncannily accurate. I would only have to touch someone and it was like a record coming through on their personality, what they were doing and what was going to happen. I had always had strange dreams that came true - premonitions.

This was different.

On one occasion, I was travelling to work by bus and the bus route took us along Roath Park Lake. This lake was a popular bird sanctuary and on the lower part of the lake pleasure boats were made available for hire. At one side, are beautiful gardens full of roses and seasonal flowers with a large greenhouse filled with exotic plants around a small pond and a waterfall. In fact, some of our wedding photographs were taken in this greenhouse. As the bus proceeded down past the lake I stared out of the window. It was early morning and a mist hung over the lake. A voice pleaded for my help. It took me by surprise. It was not a loud voice but it was like a lost soul crying out in the mist of the lake.

I looked around at the other passengers on the bus. It was fairly full but not one person showed any recognition of having heard the voice. I stared at each person waiting for a sign, as the voice pleased for help. Nothing.

The experience left me a little shaken and I arrived at work a bit dishevelled. That night I woke up sweating. I had a vivid dream. I knew who the voice belonged to and I saw that this unfortunate man had been murdered by the lake and his body thrown into its murky waters in the middle of the night.

I shivered. The experience had left me quite frightened. One thing was clear, a man was murdered, his soul was crying out for help and I had seen the whole sordid crime. I had to help.

I woke Chris up and told him what had happened and we talked. I wanted to go to the police. Chris stopped me. His logic, when you think about it is right. If I had gone to the police and they had dragged the lake and found a man's body - how did I know? The police could have looked upon this as if I had implications into the crime to know the details. If a man's body was not found - I could end up being the local nutcase. I said nothing to nobody.

Looking back, it wasn't an easy decision to make. Every morning, I travelled on that bus, I heard that poor soul crying out to be found. It was with relief two months later that he was found. I read it on a billboard lunchtime. I shook all the way back to the office. I could have helped but instead I kept quiet.

That experience left me a bit shaken to say the least and now I was ready to open up and start listening. Having experienced the lower levels, I realised I had to learn more in order to gain more knowledge.

God had given me this gift and I felt it was for a reason. I turned again to my faith and asked for guides in the spirit to help train and teach me the levels. Spirit will not help you until you ask.

I can only pray that the murdered man's family forgive me for not speaking up.

CHAPTER TWO

Mary and Philip

Istill, at this time, regularly attended church although now after having moved, was back in my old church,, All Saints, Rhiwbina. David joined the choir which he enjoyed. We settled down to a fairly normal routine of living. I must have gone up the levels in the psychic way as I was strong, strong in my faith and strong in my mind. So it was with surprise that two voices made themselves known to me and worked with me gaining my trust.

Not all the time did I hear as intuition had taken over and I felt more than heard. I felt I was being guided, to meet certain people and to read certain books.

One book made quite an impact on me. Although I only read the first two chapters, I felt that I had read what I had meant to. The book was called 'The Power of Prayer.'

It made me realise that, in effect, what had I done in my life to help the world. Nothing. I had a gift. I didn't use it. Mary was quite strong and I must admit was with me a full year. Our relationship was strong and still is. Mary guided me to the picture of 'The Light of the World' by Holman Hunt. In this picture, it shows Christ standing outside a locked door, the handle is on the inside. Christ cannot gain entry unless the door is opened from the inside.

Mary told me that to open that door, it would mean, that every sin I had committed in this life, would be brought to mind. When this happens, to ask for forgiveness from Christ for that sin and to learn where I had gone wrong, so I could learn. In my prayers, I did just that. I asked Christ into my life. Now I'm listening to a spirit who tells me what will happen, do I believe it. Well believe it. It happened.

I couldn't believe the memories that came flooding in day after day. Wow! it was true. If you don't learn, then He will certainly let you know. Try it and see.

At one stage, I was in an important meeting and all of a sudden, I saw a situation I hadn't remembered for years. It happens like that. In your most stressful times, He will test you, forgive you and love you. Mary told me that this was a process of becoming righteous. This testing, remembering and forgiveness can take a short period of time or maybe years depending upon each individual.

In my case, it took approximately three weeks. But it happened and still does to a certain extent it I don't learn.

I was now learning more about, not the church, but about how to conduct my life in respect of other people and myself. In fact, in the process, someone commented that in their opinion, my colleague was a churchgoer but I was a Christian. I'm not saying the church had it wrong, merely their teachings were not about life. This Christ taught me, that the greatest teachers of the world, lived in the real world. Sometimes, only on occasions, I heard the Master's voice.

Christmas came. I was dreading it. Living in the family house, both parents dead. I missed them. We went to midnight mass. The night was dreadful. It rained and poured. We walked to church, the rain abating for the journey. The church is about a mile away and it is a very pleasant walk. David, now around ten years old, was used to going to midnight mass and enjoyed it. On this occasion, in church, the choir come in holding a candle. It really is a beautiful service.

I was proud of my son, holding his candle, and thought of my Mum, she adored him. If only she could see him now years later. A bright, happy thoughtful child. There again, he has his moments like all kids.

The service started and the heavens opened. It bucketed down. The noise like bullets on the roof. I said to Chris a few months earlier, it would snow coming back from church after midnight mass. Something Mary had said. A present from heaven. I believed her and still did. The church roof was noisy from the heavy rain and Chris asked to get the car as we would all get soaked coming back from church. I said no - no need to, it will be snowing when we leave.

Then more minutes into the service Chris asked again - 'Please Jane, it's not going to snow, let me get the car, you'll get very wet.'

'No Chris - it's going to snow. Have faith, you'll see.'

Chris was by now getting very agitated with me and who could blame him.

'Let me get the car!' he whispered, but loud enough for the next row to hear.

I smiled and said no, it will be allright. Five minutes before the end of the service, guess what, it stopped raining. The noise on the roof subsided. And guess again, when we got outside it was snowing.

I also had another present that Christmas, which was very special. After the episode of the lake, Mary showed me how I could help - spirit rescue. One of the first spirits I helped, would you believe it, was Freddie Mercury. Freddie had died of Aids earlier in the year. I had been and still am a fan of Queen's music. Mary showed me the way.

I saw Freddie.

It was like a dream, a conscious dream, he was dressed half in black and half in white. It seemed to me he couldn't make up his mind which way to go. Half his face was black and half white. I concentrated and connected. Mary told me a way to help. By using God's white light, His pure energy, you can throw it over spirit to help guide them to the light. This I did.

I was rewarded by seeing Freddie turn all white and helped by angels to heaven. On the way up, I saw that Freddie too had angel wings.

At the time, I was told that I would receive a present at christmas from Freddie. My Christmas present, you've guessed it, Queen's last album, 'Made in Heaven.' I now meditate to this album and it works a treat. I do believe that the band were helped with that album, but not by anybody in this world.

That night, I had a strange dream and woke up with a start. It was Christmas night. Freddie had given a concert in heaven and I was asked to attend. I had seen the concert.

Freddie, in spirit, stayed with me for a short while. He was curious in the work I did, until one day, he suddenly left. Mary told me, that Freddie wanted to help and had decided to come back. She also told me, that a small ten year old boy would approach me in the future.

'Say hello, to him.' Mary said, ' and remember, you will recognise his soul. Say hello, to your friend Freddie.'

My working life was in a turmoil. The firm had been taken over by a national firm. This national firm was not doing so well in Cardiff and lost accounts. This included a very big one which I worked on. Unfortunately, I was made redundant. It didn't worry me, as I knew I would be needed elsewhere. Mary reassured me that this was the case, I enjoyed six weeks off with my son, before starting with a new firm, who had actually won that same big account. Same job, different firm. I settled down.

One day going down on the bus, Mary was emotional. I asked in my mind what was wrong.

She explained that I had reached the next level and I had learnt from her all I could. She also told me not to worry, that there were sixty four of us altogether. The sixty four were the Spiritual Teachers of the future. Mary told me the locations of every one but told me not to write it down.

'Remember,' she said. 'There are twelve of you in Great Britain alone.'

Mary told me that Philip would be taking over. I was very sad about this and asked if this was for always, or could I still talk to her. Mary didn't reply. Instead a man's voice took over.

'Mary cannot talk now she's too upset.'

At the beginning, I missed Mary and I felt that Philip did not think I was worthy of his attention. In fact, he did say he didn't know why he was with me.

But, at least, he did explain that Mary would come back and thankfully, she does from time to time. It was only after the first initial month with Philip, did I learn who Mary was. This mate of mine who I have joked with, shared my life with, was The Mary!! I couldn't believe it. Philip explained, that we all have previous lifetimes. Not every lifetime is the same, as we are all learning. Therefore, Mary had had many lifetimes and was well up todate of the world today. This time, she had chosen to be a guide. My guide, my friend, if but for a short while. So Mary might be with you - you never know. If so, love her, she's beautiful.

In those first few months of being with Philip, it was very much different. Everything seem to speed up. It was like I had to learn something and learn it fast. Philip unlike Mary, was very keen for me to learn fast. Sometimes, it was very difficult to grasp the concepts that he was bringing. So, it seems his way was by bringing people into my life.

My friends Dave, Shelia and Anne-Marie joined us for a picnic in Wiltshire. Dave enjoyed researching the unknown, especially anything to do with UFOs. Wiltshire was a well known area for UFO sightings and he had persuaded Shelia and ourselves to go to Avebury. In Avebury, there is an ancient circle of stones, in fact, the whole village seems to be in this circle.

On the way to Avebury, just outside, is a burial chamber which is suppose to be 6000 years old. We intended to have our picnic at Avebury after viewing the burial chamber. Approaching Silbury Hill, a line of cars were parked making it difficult to see where the ancient monument was to be found. We assumed it was visitors to the area as it was steeped in history, we assumed wrongly. On parking our cars further down the road it became apparent why so many visitors.

In the corn, was an indentation, which we found out from Dave, who I might add was quite excited by this find, that this was a crop circle. Origin - unknown.

Although, Dave would have us believe that the person or persons who had made it were not from this world. I was skeptic. There was a pathway alongside the crop field leading to the burial chamber. It was quite a walk and we lost the kids who wanted to investigate the phenomena.

In fact, we lost Dave too. At the top of the burial chamber was a man dowsing using two light metal rods. Dave was fascinated. He had stopped to talk.

It was fairly obvious, after twenty minutes, the man looked a bit harassed, but that has never put Dave off finding out or talking to someone he is interested in. Dave is quite harmless, but his thirst for knowledge on the paranormal, does get him into trouble, especially with his wife, Sheila.

We left him to it and the three of us decided to go through the field, to have a closer look at the crop circle.

By interconnecting lines, small and large circles were formed. The actual design looked like an insect from the road. However, close up, it was even stranger. The corn in the circles were slightly upright and not damaged, but looked although a whirlwind had somehow swirled the corn which left the design. No way could a whirlwind have made this design, which was deliberate. I have since seen a programme on the television, stating that some of the crop circles were hoaxes and man made, but after being in one I beg to differ. Something that was made in the hours of darkness, covering such a large area, with an intricate design and nobody noticing! I believe the one I was in could not be done by man but there again, who could have made them?

Coming out of the field, we were met by two range rovers pulling up. Sheila stopped to talk to the farmer whose field it was. I must add, that the burial chamber had fewer visitors than the crop field.

The farmer was furious. He told Sheila, that whoever had made the crop circle had caused damage and he was going to sue them. Farmhands spilled out of the vehicles and into the field shooing everybody out, to prevent further damage to the crop. We went back to the cars but still no Dave. Where was he? The last time we saw him was on top of the field, by the burial chamber, talking to the dowser. We waited and in the end had our picnic. About an hour later, and I might add by now one furious wife, we saw Dave running down the field chased by the farmer.

Well, Sheila's anger disappeared and like the rest of us ended up doubled up with laughter. What a sight.

We travelled on to Avebury, but as time was against us, we did what all tourists did and looked around the shops and left.

I vowed then to go back to Avebury, I was not really sure why, except Philip wanted me to.

We enjoyed our day out, but the important point of relaying this episode, was in fact, the dowser. His name was John and he was a farmer from Dorset. A couple of months later, Dave asked if John could stay, as there was a Paranormal Conference in Cardiff and John wished to attend and not knowing anybody in Cardiff, except Dave, who by now had got to know him better, asked if someone could put him up, as it was a two day conference.

As by now my interest in the paranormal was increasing, due to my own experiences, I agreed. I also asked Dave if he would mind if I joined them. Well, Philip was delighted. One thing I have learnt, is that spirit will not make decisions for you, they will help and guide, but as Philip states we still have free will. John arrived Friday night and I must add it was a convergence of like minds.

John had been to see a medium recently who told him it was important that he came to Cardiff, as he had to meet someone. That someone, you guessed, was me. After the first day at the conference, I felt elated. I met people who were so open minded, they were easy to read and was able to give such accurate readings it was untrue.

On listening to a speaker on crop circles - which I might add I was slowly taking an interest, after being inside one, John approached me with a young girl. This girl was highly distressed. Apparently, her fiancee had committed suicide and she felt his presence around her all the time.

John, without knowing me, asked me to help. I placed my hands in hers, as she was clearly so distressed. I thought that by giving her comfort, she would calm down. However, I was so surprised on touching her, that a loud mouthed youngster started shouting in my head.

'What the bloody hell does she think she's playing at. Can't she see what she's doing. Help me.'

This time, unlike the man in the lake, I knew I could. With Philip guiding, I gave her healing and reassured the young man all was well. The young girl thanked me and went back to her seat, which was immediately in front of us. The speech was interesting and quite funny and John and I remarked that the girl was now laughing. Towards the end of the speech a voice came in my head.

'Bless you, Jane, thank you.' - He was gone.

That night John and I stayed up talking to gone two in the morning. We had had very similar experiences. Similar life stories. John explained that the young girl was grieving for her lost love and felt it was her fault and in effect was keeping him on the earth plane. By healing her, the spirit of the young boy was released.

John had been dowsing for twenty years and in effect, was helping to clear and cleanse the land. He asked if I would like to learn, as he felt it was one of the reasons we had met. Philip was elated. The following morning, we went up the Wenallt, just below the reservoir was a small tumuli. On walking around the tumuli, the rods went in and out, in fact eight times. John explained these were ley lines or leys as they are known. Each ley goes in and out, therefore, there were in fact four leys. On reaching the top of the tumuli, John started praying, a prayer of healing. The Lord's Prayer is the best prayer of healing that I know.

On returning to the perimeter, on dowsing, I was amazed to see that there were now six leys, twelve times the rods went in and out. John asked if I would like to try dowsing. I agreed. It was a very strange experience, I could douse and I definitely felt the pull of the rods the same as John twelve times. In fact, I got quite excited here was something new, a form of healing on the land. John explained, that for centuries the land had been negative and in healing, it was reversing the process. However, he warned me that certain black negative leys can cause sickness if you try to heal and you are not spiritually protected. So don't try this at home folks unless you know what you are doing.

I was sorry to see John leave and we agreed to meet up again. In fact, it wasn't that long until the next meeting, but by then Philip had taught me a lot more. Philip directed me to an Ordinance Survey map of the area and as I studied it Philip helped and guided. We started with Avebury and buying a pair of rods. Since learning all this knowledge I have taught many others and have suggested to all that they buy their rods in Avebury, as it is a very special area and to say a prayer of healing as they go.

Now equipped with rods and survey map, the next step was spiritual protection. This is something that has come easy to me. Philip taught me how to bring God's Light or energy through me in colours. If you imagine God as a beautiful white light full of positive energy and then bring in that energy through your body and out through the top of your head, the crown, you are bringing God into your life. The knowledge of the positive/negative energy is centuries old - a way this race has forgotten. When the energy is positive and healed, we are healed. by using this method, you could start to heal yourself.

By bringing in a blue light, the colour can be one that you imagine is right for you, you are actually healing yourself. When first learning this pathway, you cannot heal others until you are healed yourself. On bringing the pink light of love, you will begin to love yourself. Again, you cannot love others until you learn to love yourself. After doing this process of bringing in the white, blue and pink light you may start to feel a warm feeling and tingle. Do not be afraid, the tingling is healing you. You will be experiencing the energy for yourself.

Every morning, I brought in those three colours that Philip and now Mary too was teaching. These colours were enough for me to heal the land. The very first one on the map was a small tumuli. Chris, although skeptic, agreed to take me. It turned out to be on a farmer's land. Unfortunately, at this stage, I felt the farmer would think that I was mad in saying I wanted to go into his field with metal rods to say prayers in order to heal the leys. So I'm afraid I told a little white lie and said we were historians. The farmer was most helpful, stating that the local history school teacher was also interested in the area. Apparently, a battle had taken place on the land and there was an old ruin of a windmill, which was never used as a windmill, but as a headquarters for that battle.

He showed us how to get into the field, which was through another field and Oh No! it was full of young bulls. However, unperturbed, Chris and I approached the gate. The farmer told us that if we just shooed the bulls away they would go. Chris wasn't so sure. Armed with camera and rods we gingerly opened the gate. Having lived all our lives in the city it was, in my eyes, quite brave to go shoo to a huge youngster of a bull. Shoo. It followed us. Shoo, so did the others. Shoo. We made a mad dash for the end of the field. Feeling quite brave we practically threw ourselves over the end gate. Retaining our composure, we had a look around the large field. It was fascinating.

The old windmill (see picture two) still stood standing with ivy growing all around. Inside there was quite a strange feeling. Birds had roosted at the top of the windmill and were not happy about us invading their territory. However, I knew that this was not the place. Over to the right of the field was a circle of trees. Once inside it felt right. On going around the circle of trees, the rods kept going in and out all the time. On healing, the rods stayed in. Obviously, this was quite a prominent position with views on all sides and therefore was an energy centre. On healing this centre, I felt the rush of energy and tingled all over.

Chris was kept busy the whole time taking pictures, delaying the inevitable return through the field of bulls. The bulls were by now converging at the end gate watching us. (See picture one) Curious we watching them, watching us. There seemed to be one leader of the pack and it had to be the biggest. We stayed until he lost interest and then proceeded down the field with the rest of the bulls following. Here was our chance to escape.

Felling brave, Chris asked me to walk behind him. That was until it came to the crunch and then it's every man for themselves.

I wished at that moment that John was with us, he would have known how to cope with the bulls. I felt that they were surrounding us. They were curious to know who we were and why we were in their field. However, the farmer was right. Chris waved one of the rods around and they soon changed their minds and left us alone. Again we made a dash to the end of the field where a few more bulls were gathered. It was like they were guarding our only escape route out. So, it was not quite like everyman for themselves, but nearly. The bulls didn't have time to move, we were too quick over the gate.

Looking back on that experience, the bulls did certainly seem to get more of a look in, but the important aspect of that first healing, was that it worked. Not only did it work but, I felt it. I had done something positive in my life. I felt there was no turning back.

Over the next two years, I was to investigate, realign and heal most of the leys in Cardiff and the surrounding areas. In fact, I wrote an article about the healings which was, to my delight, published.

Most of the energy centres were in prominent locations, connecting up with what I call 'sub stations' usually churches and old historical sites, where monuments have been erected. In some cases, where the leys meet our own Victorian ancestors had erected a folly, such as a made up stone circle. These stone circles, although relatively new, compared with places such as Stonehenge, can still have the same potential once healed and working.

Around Cardiff, I have located approximately six energy centres and I think that it is no mistake that Castle Coch is built over one centre. The keep in Cardiff Castle is a centre and the owners of the Castle, the Bute family, erected a stone circle on the ground outside the Clock Tower. (See picture three) This redirected the energy to the Clock Tower, the top room has a most unusual designed floor. The centre of that floor is a picture of the world. The energy has been redirected to that picture.

I went along to heal Cardiff Castle, (See picture four) but prior to the healing, Philip wanted me to see someone. In doing this work John was correct about spiritual protection, as on many occasions, I had felt the negative/dark side and still do today. In simple terms, the devil, but not as you imagine or as the church would have you believe. I have had many experiences since in respect of the devil which crop up later in the book. Today, Philip wanted me to see a psychic. This psychic worked a few days a week in an arcade over a small crystal shop.

This psychic was seeing people with depression and suicidal tendencies, which if he was unprotected, would experience the emotions of these people and get depressed himself. So on my way to the Castle I called in.

The psychic picked up himself that I was not there for a reading, but to help him. He listened.

I explained about the colours and how to bring in the white light of God. Finally, one of the ways Philip had taught me to protect myself, was to bring down a pyramid of gold over and under yourself. On bringing this pyramid down state in your mind 'I bring down the golden pyramid of protection.' Fill this pyramid with God's white light over and under you. The emotions of disturbed or negative people will not effect you. If you should feel that you are being psychically attacked, place mirrors on the outside of the pyramid and this will, in effect, rebound back to the source attacking.

In this work, I have been psychically attacked many times. I feel it. It usually starts with a headache and a feeling of depression. On one occasion, I felt every thought I had was negative. I knew I was being psychically attacked. Now I welcome it, as I know if I visit somewhere and this happens, I'm in the right place.

I healed Cardiff Castle and the energy, although still strong in the Clock Tower, is now back where it belongs. On this occasion, I had to attend the tour around the castle. In front of a crowd of people, I discretely stepped on the picture of the world and proceeded with the prayer work, whilst the tour guide was explaining the history of the room. I don't think anybody noticed, or if they did, they didn't say anything to me.

Our Victorian ancestors knew this knowledge and used that energy. How to use that energy and why, I explain later in the book.

These centres are very strong and after being inside them for years, I now tingle whenever I am near one. The leys criss-cross the country, however, there are certain dominant lines which meet at a lower more central point.

For example, one dominant line starts on the Ordnance Survey map number 171 just outside Tinkinswood at Long Cair Stones. This connects with the remains of a Roman Villa through Pontcanna Church on to Rhymey Castle coming out of Cardiff again through the centre of another church in Marshfield.

I have actually healed all these sites mentioned and the dominant line is now working. But what is interesting is that another dominant line coming down from Ystrad cutting through Rhiwbina, Wenallt also meets at Pontcanna church. Although Pontcanna church is a definite energy centre and quite a strong one, it is up for sale at the time of writing this book.

I feel compelled to say, that the healing of this church was not an easy matter. I felt warned off the site for a long time and felt very uneasy, until completing the actual healing.

The energy is a natural force, which has been negative, as it has not been husbanded for centuries. But, it is obvious, that our ancestors knew the importance of this energy, which can be used for negative or positive purposes. The 'sub stations' as stated are usually churches etc. and I feel, that I am going onto a very controversial subject, but I must add, that most of the churches needed healing. My son and I can tell you the time when a service is taking place at our local church as both of us tingle. This energy can be used in many ways. When a person goes to church he/she is spiritually uplifted and feels great. The energy is being used positively.

In the evenings, I would get out the map and start linking the centres and leys together, giving a criss-cross pattern. Philip, at this stage, was always helping and guiding giving me more colours to learn and over the period of time explaining what each one meant and it's purpose.

Chris was still skeptic at the work I did, but accepted it. On all our visits there was usually something of interest for him. On one occasion, a sheep dog trial which was held just for him, as visiting farmers were on the way to a competition and gave their dogs a warm up to show Chris. On another occasion, the ruins we went to was a large field where model aeroplanes were flying. I believe that spirit gave Chris some interest in most locations, so he didn't mind helping me.

Then out of the blue one morning, Philip said quite emotionally, he was no longer to be with me for a short while. He, like Mary, had taught me the next step. I was very surprised but he added that he would be back, if I so wished. In meditation, I have seen both Mary and Philip, they were nothing like I had imagined. Both were young, dressed in old fashioned chainmail solder's outfits. On top, was a white tunic with a large gold cross on. Always, in meditation, I had seen myself in the same tunic but with a red cross.

That night, a celebration.

When I meditate, there is a church, a beautiful white cathedral, which is carved out of a white marble cliff face. It is a very large cathedral, with beautiful stained glass. On this occasion, I saw My Master, My Lord, who gave me the gold cross. It seems that, although Philip and Mary are no longer guiding me, I have learnt that they will be there when I ask for them. They are now guiding others. Philip stated, that at the beginning he didn't think I was worthy of his attention, but at the end, we became quite attached. He loved me and was sorry I had to move on. So here I am without a guide, a soldier of Christ.

At every healing, of any ley or energy centre, I call on God's white light, which I now see as a tunnel. People have stated that they see this tunnel when they have near death experiences, or in meditation. I only have to close my eyes and it is always there. When I call on the white light, I always release trapped spirits wherever I go. I ask My Father, to release the trapped spirits and for those spirits to go towards the white light, not to be afraid, they will be with their loved ones, their family and friends. Most of this I feel. I now feel spirit around me, whether good or bad, negative or positive, light or darkness.

I felt alone.

I knew if I asked, they would be there. There must be a reason, there usually is. In meditation, Mary and Philip were still there, but is now obvious their job is finished.

John telephoned.

I described what happened. He was interested in the outfits, it sounded like the Nights Templar. So, I researched the Nights Templar. A new programme had come out about the Holy Grail and The Nights Templar and it certainly is an eye opener. I feel that there is more that what I am led to believe.

John asked if I would like to see the medium in Dorset. I agreed, as Dave too decided he would like to visit her. So to Dorset. This is where I first heard my new guide. Well, he came as a surprise to me, as now I was going on a very strange path indeed.

My new guide was Merlin.

CHAPTER THREE

Merlin

I could write a book on it's own about Merlin. He is the most wonderful, beautiful, mischievous, witty, loving know-all I know. I love him. Don't get me wrong I loved Mary and Philip but Merlin - what a character. When I least expect it, there he is in my ear telling me all sorts of stories. In fact, I think one day, I will write that book. But today, Merlin is with me and is helping to write this chapter which is important - so he is serious today.

Another family outing, this time to Dorset, with out friends, Dave and Sheila.

We dropped the kids off at one of the new type of leisure centres, which has a play pool with loads of tunnels. I almost wished that I could have joined them. Some of these tunnels went outside the building, it looked great fun.

Dave and I had decided to see the medium John told us about and have a reading. I was in for an eye opener.

The medium and her husband had rented a cottage just outside Dorchester. This cottage, although seemed in the country, was not far from the town, but very pretty. The energy I felt. It was healed. In fact, the medium explained, a ley went through the cottage. The husband was interested in crop circles and we had a very interesting discussion. Out of nowhere came knowledge about the crop circles that I couldn't possibly have known. I automatically knew how they were made and why. I surprised myself. He thought that I must have researched the subject, but I hadn't apart from the one lecture in the conference, which was more on the composition of the wheat and the side effects.

I knew someone was guiding me.

I went into a back room, which was a small dining room, to see the medium. The conversation that took place was taped. I still have the tape. She told me that I had many lifetimes of doing the work I am now doing, working with the colours. Once in Atlantis as a priestess, another in Egypt again as a priestess working with all the knowledge.

She went on to say, I was a healer in not only the physical but also of the mind.

I had many lives as ordinary people, in order to learn. But my job on earth on this occasion was one which I had chosen. Apparently, I had chosen to come back to teach, preach and heal. She told me that I had come as an angel on a blue beam of light, to help the earth and that I was not alone.

There were in fact sixty four of us. I couldn't believe it, Mary had told me that. Was it true? Each of us had chosen to come back and we were, in effect, the Spiritual Teachers of the future. At one stage, I had a lifetime as Count St Germain who had the knowledge of eternal youth, which apparently, I know! I'll let you know when I find out.

The medium went on to say, that on one occasion, I lived as a monk who deviated from the norm. This in effect was the work I was doing now or would do in the future putting right what I had done wrong in the past. Nice one, me a monk and how did I deviate? However, she was right about one thing, I could heal and I did see and hear.

In previous months, I was woken up in the middle of the night and two lights in the shape of people were standing by my side of the bed. I heard, but not as a spoken word.

'She's waking up, come.' I was not afraid, I felt strangely calm and watched them leave the bedroom.

The medium explained that I was being visited in order that I could learn. These light beings were teaching me when I slept. Apparently, I was a light being, a cosmic light being. The tape is about an hour long and explains more about past lives. This fascinated me. People who are regressed, explain in detail about past lives. The medium asked for healing, which I gave. I left there with many thoughts going around in my head. Little did I know that I was to experience those past lives and what I had done wrong. More importantly, this lifetime put it right.

Dave also had a fascination about past lives. He has a natural talent and is able to hypnotise people. He tried once with Chris and I, which was not very successful. However, he has had many successes in this field and each time past lives have come up.

So when another conference in Cardiff was to be held about the paranormal, Dave acquired tickets for us all to go. Sheila was not too happy about it and decided to stay away. This was due to the fact a lot of the speakers were talking about UFOs, which really I was not interested in, but I was interested in meeting more open minded people. The last conference, I felt was important in not what was said, but who you met. So I agreed. Chris and Sheila decided not to go. Another bonus was that John from Dorset decided to come across and attend and as always I enjoyed his company.

At the conference, I met many people. Some affected me psychically. I knew they were negative and they gave me a headache, so much so, that I decided to leave one speaker. Her speech on UFOs was not the reason, I could feel her drawing on the audience, drawing their energy. She gave me a very bad headache.

I left and went upstairs and decided to look around the side stalls. One of the side stalls was selling crystals. The stall holder looked at me and gave me a seat.

She told me that I was the second person to come to her during this speaker.

'Help yourself.' She said. 'You know you can, you are a healer.'

I sat down and brought in the energy and then protected myself. I looked at the stall holder and thanked her. She went on and said a very strange think.

'You are a light from the cosmos.'

First the medium in Dorset and now this stallholder.

I practically ran from her, but she was right, she knew I could heal myself. This left me thinking all kinds of things, who was I and what did it all mean. Again, I gave readings at this conference to help others but still the stall holder's words were echoing in my mind.

Also, at the conference, I met a girl called Theresa. Theresa helps run a spiritual group in Mountain Ash, which is about thirty miles outside Cardiff. This group run a shop which also incorporates spiritual healing. Something I was getting more and more into.

I came away with more questions than answers. Pondering on these questions, I was drawn to a leaflet from the conference about the Sir Isaac Newton Conference in 1993 and felt compelled to write. I wrote a small article.

This article gave the ABC.

In other words, it simplified a complicated theory. What I didn't know then, but I do now, is that Merlin was with me. His thoughts, his teachings are always ABC. That phrase he uses all the time.

A scientific disaster took place when Sir Isaac Newton's model of the universe was discarded and replaced by Einstein's Theory of

Relativity.

Apart from in Russia and a few heretics in the West, the whole of orthodox science is locked into a largely false and hopelessly outdated scientific theory.

Dr Louis Essen D.Sc, FRS, OBE, is the inventor of the atomic clock. For trying to bring common sense back into physics he was told further such activity would place the tenure of his post in jeopardy.

Many of the world great scientists have come from the ranks of engineers, Ronald Pearson (from Bath) has completely discarded Einstein's outdated Theory of Relativity and by making a couple of additions to Sir Isaac Newton's physical laws has matched up with quantum mechanics which provides a totally satisfactory solution of quantum gravitation.

Mr Pearson attended the Newton Conference in 1993 and his scientific paper has been well received and published. This outstanding British scientist is recognised in Russia but not in his own country as he is censored in his own country.

Pauli predicted that there may well be particles within the atom other than the proton, electron and the recently discovered neutron that would revolutionise scientific thinking. We have now discovered over 200 subatomic particles making up our physical universe coming under the general heading of quarks and leptons. In order to discover the etheric world Mr Pearson has taken a step further and pointed out that everything we have discovered so far within the atom is being produced from smaller primary particles at a sub quantum level.

A paper written by R D Pearson 'Key to Consciousness - Quantum Gravitation' shows that a primary consciousness lies at a sub quantum level of reality; in the invisible.

In simple terms, or as Merlin states, the ABC, Einstein forgot to take into account the energy force of the apple thrown. Everything in the Universe contains energy. Newton's theory took this into account and by estimating the energy force of the particle in question the law of gravitation is taken one step further into the invisible.

We cannot see radio waves with the naked eye, but we know they exist. Newton's theory of Ether proves the invisible, which opens up a new field of research into the so called paranormal phenomena.

Merlin likes to give me confirmation of what I learn so he directed me to a book called 'The Celestine Phrophercy.' I was amazed to learn that not only did I know the insights, but I could have written the sequel.

By this time, Merlin had also directed me to the spiritual tarot cards. Now being a Christian, I felt this was very wrong. For quite a few months I pondered about this request. When I went to visit the psychic, in Cardiff, he too used tarot cards, which I felt was right for him, but not for me. Earlier on, I did use the ordinary cards but that was only playing, Merlin was serious. So, in the end, I bought a pack, of course, the pack was not chosen by me.

For the next two or three months Merlin taught me the cards. I have to admit they do answer your questions and they give me more of an insight into people's own spiritual path. I use them to help people and to learn, by way of confirmation, that what I am doing is right or wrong. As these are spiritual tarot, there are no bad cards. There are four suits e.g. wind - intellect; fire - spiritual; water - emotional and earth - material. There are twenty six players depicting many realms of life.

I have to admit that they have taught me a lot. One particular card gave me a lot of trouble learning until Merlin directed me to a book in the local library 'Meditation on the Spiritual Tarot' which was written by a priest!!

The next step he taught me was about Karma, The Cosmic Law of Karma. Whatever you do in life, will come back on you. Do not deny the consequences of your actions. Everybody is responsible for their thoughts, words and deeds. For even thought constitutes action in the energy cycles of the universe. Don't be deceived. God is not mocked, for whatever a man soweth, then so shall he also reap.

Unfortunately, the above has been proved over and over again to me. Frightening isn't it. Merlin says our minds are like sewers. I know he reads mine because he answers me in the cards. Responsible for every thought, word and deed. Wow!

Even more frightening is the fact that we are accountable, for not only the sins that we do in this lifetime, but in past lifetimes. Have you ever been to a place and recognised it, but you don't know how, as you have never been there before. Have you ever met someone and instantly tell them your life story and you don't know why. Do you click with some people and others you can't stand, although you have never met them before. Do you feel that inside something is happening to you, but you don't know what and you cannot quite understand why.

Well where do I start.

The energy in a lot of areas in Great Britain has been changed and is now positive. I am not the only one doing this work, there are others who have learnt this knowledge, but not from any book or person. People will now be picking up on that positive energy and will be thinking quite out of character.

In our lifetimes, we have been many things. God had introduced time, in order for us to learn. When we die we go to God, or to our Soul Group and understand the things that we did wrong in the last lifetime. When we come back, reincarnated, we try to put right those things we have done wrong. That is why you are drawn to others as maybe they are part of your Soul Group, in this physical lifetime. Each time we sleep we connect with our higher soul in order for us to learn and to remember what it is that we have come back to do. This is called original sin. When we come into this life time we have original sin and as we live our lives we accumulate more sin.

So, the first step is to make yourself righteous and the next step is to eradicate original sin. Each person can have as many as one, to Oh! I don't know how many, but Merlin states that if you have around twelve or so on, you are going the wrong way - negative.

One of the gifts I have been given, is to know how many sins each and every person has. In effect, I am allowed to tell that person, that is if they are interested, remember we still have free will, where they should go to eradicate a sin. Although, I understand all of this because I have actually been through it and eradicated my sins, it is a very difficult concept to understand for the ordinary person in the street.

So, here goes, as Merlin says, the ABC. The best way is to tell you of my own experiences.

Castle Morgraig

Built on a ridge at the south edge of the Glamorgan uplands, Castle Morgraig was well sited for a border defence and look-out for the Welsh territory. The ridge offers uninterrupted views south across the coastal plain to Cardiff, the Severn estuary and Somerset beyond. It was built in 1267 in an attempt to stem Llywelyn's growing threat to the Glamorgan lowlands by Earl Gilbert of Clare. Gilbert began the construction of a massive fortress at Caerphilly rendering Castle Morgraig obsolete.

That is what your historians say about Castle Morgraig, which was owned by a Welsh Prince. I know different. Castle Morgraig is actually, as the crow flies, about one mile from my house. The year before last my son, David, got very friendly with a young boy staying in the area and going to the same school. Nathanial was from Boston, America and his parents were history teachers who had taken six months off from school to actually learn about Great Britain for themselves and to take the knowledge back with them. I saw them regularly over the summer, as Nathanial went camping with David and guess where they went camping - Castle Morgraig. (See Picture five)

I didn't take the hint to go and look for myself. It only hit me that one of my original sins was committed in Castle Morgraig, when after Nathanial returned to this country for a short stay and looked us up again. Nathanial's father had taken a beautiful picture of trees around Castle Morgraig and gave me one as a memento. David had been talking about the castle for some time. I decided to pay a visit.

Armed with rods, we left the car in the Public House car park where at the end was a sty to enter the field. This is where the castle ruins were situated. This was farm land and the sheep were grazing in the field. They were curious to see what we were up to. No I'm allright with sheep, it's only young bulls that worry me.

On this occasion, I asked the rods for the direction of where I should be. The rods stopped immediately before the entrance of the castle ruins. Again, I asked for direction. The rods pointed to a ditch that runs up to the main building. At the bottom of the ditch, the rods came together indicating I was in the right place. I said the Lord's Prayer. On bringing in the white light, I felt as though I was being watched, but not by any physical being.

'Dear Father, with your beautiful white light, heal the leys, heal the energy.'

I was being surrounded. I closed my eyes and saw them. Twenty maybe twenty-five figures surrounding me. Some were dressed as knights, others in old twelfth/thirteenth century peasant costumes. I went on.

'Spirits trapped go towards the white light, do not be afraid.'

At that moment, a white beam came down from the sky and they all looked towards the light.

'You will be with your loved ones, your family, your friends.'

I was rewarded by seeing them leave me and walking towards the light they ascended.

What an experience. I though great my job is done. Little did I know what was to happen next. Chris was in the main building by the keep. I climbed out of the ditch and walked towards him, only to be stopped. Fear grabbed my heart. I felt it first, then saw. Such overwhelming evil, such a feeling of dread. Something really bad happened in this place. What I had seen and what had grabbed my arm was a bloody knight. I just knew, this was to do with one of my original sins. I stood before a knight I had murdered. Summing up all my courage. I started to speak in my mind to the knight.

'Forgive me.'

I said the Lord's Prayer again. 'Dear Father in Heaven, forgive me my sin, release the trapped spirit.'

I felt remorse. Suddenly, the energy was released and he was free. Wow! not only do you feel your sin, you actually know what you have done wrong. There was more to come. Chris was standing in the ruins of a tower, he was praying, something I very rarely see, as he is a very private person. I climbed up to where he stood. Chris opened his eyes, ' I think this was a bedroom.' He said and walked off. It was. I closed my eyes and saw the most beautiful woman dressed in a long flowing gown.

She was obviously a lady. On her head was a strange long hat attached to her hair. She was so sad. I felt connected with her somehow. Still to this day, I don't know who she was, but on releasing the spirits trapped in the main building she was the last to leave. I watched them ascend.

At the top, where it goes out of my view, the lady turned round and waived at me. I will never forget that moment or that vision of pure loveliness.

In all, it took about half an hour to do the work and to heal the energy. To my surprise, there were two energy centres. This indeed is a very strong place. I felt that for my part it was over. My heavy heart was now filled with joy.

I relaxed. My heart started beating at a normal rate. Then as soon as I was relaxed, I felt another spirit, I nearly jumped out of my skin, as it was so sudden. But Merlin is like that always in a rush. Sometimes, I wish he would slow down. Merlin explained that in certain special places there is a holy artefact to be found. These artefacts are kept in the spirit world until the key has been turned. The key are the souls of those people to which the place is connected. Merlin went on to say that there was a book in Castle Morgraig to be found and this book would only be released when all the souls of those connected had visited the place. Their energy, along with others, is the key to turning the lock.

Merlin also told me that Castle Morgraig was connected to the house where we lived and I would see a difference very soon. In fact, it took about two hours. I had already opened up the house and healed the energy. On releasing the energy at the castle it had poured into all the 'sub stations' etc via the leys. I felt the surge, it was wonderful. On getting out the Ordinance Survey Map, I realised that I was actually living on an energy centre myself. My house connected up to the Wenallt, Pontcanna, The Windmill Site, another site to the west where a Roman Fortress was and Castle Morgraig.

Since I had started doing the healing work, I always tingled and felt the energy, but in the house now it vibrated. The very point of the energy centre is at the bottom of the stairs in the hall.

Merlin went on to tell me that God places you in the right place at the right time. I am only one mile away from the castle. So look around you. Maybe you are drawn to a certain place near you, if you are, it does not harm to say the Lord's Prayer there.

If you are restless and you wish to move and you don't know why, then perhaps these words make sense. Rely on your intuition, your inner voice, perhaps God in His infinite wisdom is trying to let you know where to go.

John from Dorset telephoned.

He told me that Susan, a farmer's wife, wished to visit me and was it allright if they came down the following weekend. Oh delight, to see John again. The more we met, the more we didn't have to talk. It was like we both knew what the other was thinking. Susan must be special, as he didn't usually bring anybody with him.

John and Susan arrived early on the Saturday morning. Being a farmer, John always arrived well prepared and out came the sandwiches. Susan was thin, just looking at her worried me. Susan was an American, who had come over to this country and married a farmer. On her first visit to this country, she was drawn to a particular area that she'd never seen before. After going to a healing service in America she had seen a vision of a Norman church. She knew it was in that area, but when she saw the church it was Victorian and in the wrong place. Further down the road from the Victorian church was a ruin of smaller Norman church.

Susan knew this was the right place and knew she had to do penance at this church and an act of constriction for a sin she had committed in a previous lifetime. She had crawled on her knees to the middle of the ruin and could not get up until she had experienced penance.

Susan had given up a good career in America to come to this country and my heart went out to her. She had four original sins left and needed help. I taught her to dowse and how to bring in God's energy in the three colours, God's white light; pink of love and blue of healing. At the beginning she had problems in dowsing but by giving her some of my energy was successful.

I also did her tarot cards and saw that her soul was in torment and needed direction. She had understood herself she needed to come to Wales, but she didn't know why and where.

I also saw she was connected to Castle Morgraig. So back to the castle we went. This time Chris didn't come, but our friend Dave was interested, so he came. Over the sty and bang, Susan was in a right state. I was really worried and was deciding whether to get her out of there. She didn't look very strong to start with.

But no, she was determined to carry on. This time Susan was using my rods to find out the answers. All I could do at each stop was to help. She felt everything. At each stop she was getting weaker. After the fourth one, I felt enough was enough, she couldn't take much more. Could I help her, I asked spirit. No, came the reply. At the fifth, Oh great joy, she was released and as she slowly recovered she explained all that had happened and what she had felt.

So, the historians say Castle Morgraig was obsolete. Well historians, I can tell you three people who have all experienced the same thing. A large battle went on there and it was inhabited. One confirmation did take place. John is psychic and picks up like me. I was so concerned about Susan at Castle Morgraig that I didn't talk to John and Dave until we got back to the house. John Stated.

'Did you know that the spirit of Merlin has been in that castle.'

'Yes John, he came with me last weekend.'

Our guests stayed for a meal and what a celebration. Halfway through the meal the energy surge came. It hit me with surprise as somebody else had healed this time. Joy of joy, John felt it too. We had our meal out on the patio and I was able to explain more to Susan about Original Sin, the energy and of course where she had to go next.

All of this can be confirmed by the person you are teaching, as once they pick up the energy they can usually dowse. If you can dowse, you can ask questions as you will get either a yes or no answer. So, everything I teach can be confirmed by the pupil. In this case, Susan's next original sin was in York and this was confirmed by her own dowsing.

Unfortunately, if you ask any questions for material gain, such as the lottery numbers, Oh No, no such luck - they will not work. Believe me, because I've tried.

One person I taught asked a question for material gain and was pushed backwards. Be warned. God is not mocked, for whatsoever a man soweth, that shall he also reap. Remember Karma.

I explained to John and Dave about the coincidences I had experienced, especially with the fact that I knew I was different. I had always been a loner and the spiritual pathway was familiar to me. I felt different and was concerned with, who I was and what I was. These worries left me doubting myself. It certainly felt a very strange path, one that I was not used to. Having attended church most of my life, everything that I was doing seemed against their teaching. I really felt that I needed confirmation that what I was doing was right and was God's way.

Everybody should question if they feel it is wrong and I was questioning. Always, I return to prayer. On this occasion, I asked for a sign that I was doing His work.

CHAPTER FOUR

The Wondrous Cross

It's Saturday morning, it's windy and pouring with rain. The leaves are falling and winter is fast approaching. Towards the end of October, a couple of years ago something truly amazing happened and I have been woken up this morning at 7.00 am to write this chapter. As I sit in the kitchen, having my first cup of coffee of the day, I ponder on why I have been woken up so early. At first, I thought it was Merlin. Strange Merlin now wakes me up with a kiss.

A couple of weeks ago I overslept for work. A loud voice shouted in my head, 'Jane.' I raised my head off the pillow only to be kissed. It startled me for a second, as I really felt it. On realising the time, I quickly got ready for work. On the bus there was Merlin. So it was you. Now when he comes to me, as a form of confirmation that it is him, I feel tingling on my lips and sometimes a kiss.

This morning was different. This chapter I am about to write is an important one and on drinking that cup of coffee, I realised, I wouldn't be on my own writing it.

Well, who is it. I said. Philip. Came back the reply. I was delighted, I hadn't heard from Philip for a long while.

'I love you, Philip.'

An overwhelming feeling of joy entered me. ' I love you to bits, Jane. Do the cards for confirmation.' I did as I was asked, they told me I was enlightened that I was not alone and that I was seeing clearly.

Philip is helping me with this chapter, as he states he was with me during this memorable period.

Dave telephoned, 'Remember Theresa in Mountain Ash - you know you met her at the conference.'

'Ah Yes.' I replied.

Dave went on. 'Well her group are having a spiritual meeting, would you like to go, they have asked to see you.'

So on a dark cold but clear night, I went to Mountain Ash with Dave. As this was a spiritual group, I was hoping to get some answers. But on the way I was told tonight I was to be the teacher. I disbelieved, as I really by now was looking for confirmation that I was doing the right thing, God's work.

If I am to be the teacher tonight, please Lord, give me a sign that I am doing the right thing. Always I return to prayer.

We arrived at a terraced house, which I understood was one of the member's of this group. Theresa opened the door and immediately flung her arms around me. I found out that Theresa is a bit like Dave, she believed in UFOs, but also saw the spiritual side. She believed she was not from this earth. I was drawn to Theresa, but I knew I was her teacher and whether she believed this, I don't know. Theresa was also psychic and could pick up on people.

We went into the front room which was filled with people but space was made for us to sit down. We were made very welcome. Theresa talked bout the group and what they were doing. Forgive me, darling Theresa, but realise I was not on my own as Philip states he was with me, I took over the meeting.

At certain times, especially when I am not alone, I am unbelievably strong. Strong in character and in what I am saying. Knowledge comes automatically. A knowledge I myself cannot know. I do believe that it was Philip who took over that meeting.

One by one I asked the group who they were and what they were doing. I don't believe in coincidences anymore. I believe that all of us are guided, whether we know it or not. So pay attention to what you are thinking and doing as one day you may think things you could not possibly know and surprise yourself. We are not alone.

I then proceeded to show them how to bring in God's white light. I was delighted to hear that some of the group had already been taught this knowledge. I helped and guided until it was time to leave. I had met some beautiful people. On leaving, I was stopped - it was Carol. Carol I saw was already full of God's love.

She explained that recently two boys had drunk themselves into a stupor and felt they had died. She helped them and they recovered. Was it true? she enquired. I told her I saw God's pink light of love. She looked pleased.

'It was the pink light I threw over them.' she replied.

'Then you are right.'

Carol was a healer, a strong healer. I could see that in the future she would be called upon many times to heal. I told her so and she was delighted. Dear Lord, use me as a vessel of Your Peace.

We left quite late and Dave was worried about Sheila. As we were not far from his home, he asked if we could stop to see if Sheila was all right. I agreed, I was in no rush. I told Dave on the way that I had asked for a sign, confirmation that I was doing God's work. I have now more questions than answers. Philip was right, that night I was the teacher.

Dave lives outside Pontypridd, high up in the clouds as I call it. His bungalow is nearly at the top of a mountain and the view is amazing. The night was clear and the sky looked magnificent as I stood in the driveway.

Suddenly, out of nowhere, lights were going on and off. One light appeared and then left the sky. Another one appeared in a different place and disappeared again. Obviously, something was trying to get our attention.

'Look at the sky Dave.'

He was astonished, small lights were winking at us. Dave immediately went into his kitchen, he was very excited, he was getting his video camera.

As soon as Dave went into his kitchen, the sky lit up with a cross. My mouth flew open, I just starred. The cross was huge, it was heavenly - I had my sign.

When Dave came back out the cross had disappeared. I told him about what I had seen, Oh! ever so calmly, but inside I was elated. I am sure the serene calmness I felt was something to do with what I had seen.

I felt different. I was different. I knew I was doing God's work. On the return journey, I was quiet. I think looking back, I was in a state of shock. I still don't understand how I took it so calmly. My whole being was doing cartwheels and in writing this, I just feel very emotional. It did happen. I have seen the sky light up with God's cross. What a sight. What an unforgettable memory.

If ever I doubt now, I remember that sign. It is always natural for anyone to doubt. If you are uncertain ask for your sign of confirmation. If you dowse, ask if I am right, you will have your answer. If you like, you can also ask if what I have written is true, again, I have no doubts you will have your answer.

John telephoned. He was on his way to Ireland and wished to stop off on his return journey. Could he stay. Of course, John is always welcomed, even by Chris who is still skeptic. Chris enjoyed John's company. He was going to Ireland to help someone move back to Wiltshire and this person was elderly and unwell, he decided to help.

John said this would be in a few weeks time. Meanwhile, Dave had asked could we climb a mountain near him, as he wanted the energy to be healed around him. Me climb a mountain!! In the past year I had taken up swimming to help get fit, as I was putting on weight, but I was doubtful whether I could climb a mountain. Little did I know that before that Christmas, I was to climb two and the second one was treacherous as it was covered with snow.

'Yes Dave, of course I will.'

So one day in November of that year, Chris and I dressed warmly. I must be mad. We met Dave in Pontypridd and taking the two cars proceed to the mountain. We left the cars at the bottom of a very steep incline. With many stops on the way, we reached the top of this steep incline. The going then was not too bad but the ground was hard and rugged. It certainly was a very wild place and the wind didn't help.

Half way up we met a local farmer with his sheepdog. I have noticed when ever I do my work, I always meet people who help direct me to the right place. In addition, I also have signs, signs in nature too.

The farmer stopped to talk. He told us that he regularly took this walk as it was so beautiful. Beautiful, I was still recovering from the climb to talk. This farmer put me to shame, here I was a young person out of breath and the farmer must have been a good twenty years older, but he showed no sign of strain. I must get fit. He showed us the way to the summit and warned us to be careful as some of the cracks were very deep into the mountain. That's all I need, can we go down now, please, pretty please.

I can now feel Merlin back with me as I write. You can tell the difference, his wit comes through.

How I got to the summit, I don't know. As I've said I'm given strength when I most need it. But it was worth it. The view took my breath away or was it the wind?

From the summit you could see the Brecon Beacons. On all sides you saw literally for miles. The summit was quite small and to the right was a ditch. Dave had taken his video camera and filmed the healing. I felt this was a very special place. I closed my eyes and saw a circle of stones, a bit like Stonehenge, but smaller. This was a ceremonial place which has not been used for centuries.

On healing, I closed my eyes again. I saw the white light travel like a bullet opening up all the leys and the energy centres for miles. I felt the rush of energy and as it hit me, I felt elated. It was like, well the closest I can say, is euphoria, I was in heaven.

The climb down was a lot better. Dave took us to another site, the other side of the valley, called Heads of the Valley. Here was a reservoir surround by mountains, magnificent. I stood on a stone which had a prominent view over the land. Again I did my healing. Again, euphoria. Wow! what a job.

On the way back I was exhausted, a voice - it was Philip.

'Do you realise Jane that you don't have to get out of the car to do the healing. If you ask The Lord to heal every ley and energy centre as you travel, it will happen. Try it and see.'

So on the way back, I did try it and behold it did happen. Chris must have thought me mad. Here I was with hand up, palm open to the mountains and valleys as we journeyed home. Each ley and energy centre which opened up I was rewarded by a surge of energy through my feet. I felt it all. Now wherever I walk and I feel that surge of energy I know another ley has been healed.

I vowed to get fit. So back to swimming. In the health club that my firm had joined, I had made many friends. One friend, Hilary, had problems and she came to me. Hilary was suffering from nightmares. For a long time she had not slept properly. I told her about my healing work and would she be interested. If so, perhaps she would like to come to the house for a session.

Hilary readily agreed. Hilary was also suffering from a lack of confidence and I felt that the nightmares were the cause. Hilary also felt that something had happened to her and this was the cause of her nightmares.

Chris joined us for the healing session. Prior to the session, I prepared. The preparation always start with prayers. I also did the cards. The Hermit came out. The Hermit means that in your own heart you carry the light and love you have often seek outside yourself. Each one of us holds the power to fulfil ourselves from within. Celebrate and accept yourself as one connected to the whole but also as an individual worthy and magnificant. At this precise time you may feel alone. Believe me, no one is ever alone. Raise up your inner light and place it on a mountain top where everyone can see it. As a guide, you can aid the seekers who come your way. Remember, a lamp is not made to hide under a bushel.

Hilary arrived and we went into the back room. This room I use for most of my work.

The back room has a lovely view over our long garden and as I sit typing, I can look out now and then to see God's beauty.

I sat next to Hilary and Chris sat opposite.

Hilary started to explain that she was suffering from a reoccurring nightmare which woke her up. Each time she dreamed she saw more and more and what she had seen was frightening her. She could remember lights and she felt she was being experimented on. In fact, the whole experience had led her to believe she was suffering from an alien abduction. Well, the subject of UFOs had cropped up due to Dave's interest but, I was still skeptic on whether we were being visited.

I explained that one of the gifts I have been given was to be able to record, something like a video recorder, what a person sees. So, in effect, if I touched her hands, I would experience what she was experiencing.

On explaining the above Hilary readily agreed. She wanted to learn the truth.

I held her hands and immediately pictures formed in my mind. As Hilary relayed her dream, I saw it. At one stage, I could see her in a field of yellow flowers dressed in a yellow, flowing gown dancing, flying, enjoying her freedom. Another time, I saw the earth as a far away place and Hilary was flying around, as if celebrating. She was on her own.

Hilary talked us through a stage where she came back to earth and walking again through this field of yellow flowers there was a cave entrance. Then she was flying off again, she explained.

'Ahh! hang on Hilary, come back to that cave entrance again.' I said coldly.

'Cave entrance, Oh yes. No, you don't want to go in there.' Hilary replied.

'Oh yes I do, come back to the cave entrance Hilary.'

Hilary had her eyes closed, I could see she was distressed.

'No. Let's go and play in the field of flowers.'

The pictures I was receiving returned to the field of flowers again. I hadn't seen a cave entrance, I saw a spaceship!

Hilary's mind had rejected the spaceship as not plausible and had replaced it with a cave entrance, she would recoil and go off somewhere else. This toing and froing went on for about five minutes. I knew if she was to get over her experience she had to go through it. I felt I was being cruel, but I was being guided all the time.

At last she went into the cave, only I didn't see a cave. The tunnel she was in was a passageway into a main room which was domed. It looked like grey/black marble. I saw the beings with her, they were surprisingly like all the other stories of abductions, small grey with large eyes. In the middle of the room was a table. This is hurting me to go on. Poor Hilary. I felt annoyed, very frustrated.

Like a flash, our minds were connected and Hilary carried on with her story. Everything she was relaying now was the same as what I was seeing.

She explained that she was being experimented on, but felt nothing as her soul was out of her body and it was like she was floating over the scene and it was not really happening to her. She saw her mutilated body below and prayed that these beings could put her back together again properly. She sent out the feeling of love to her mutilators. I was crying and so was Hilary. At one of these sessions, I feel everything that the other person is going through.

Chris, who was watching the whole thing, felt for both of us. Afterwards, he explained that as we were going through the experience, he put God's Pyramid of Protection over us - and this coming from a skeptic!

Afterwards, I healed her. I explained about the energy and bringing in God's colour of white, pink and blue to help heal herself.

After she left, I was so confused. Hilary did go through that experience. Does that mean that all the stories I have heard about UFOs are true. Did they really exist, if so, who were they and what were they doing here. This was the first time this has happened and I must admit, it wasn't very pleasant. It also opened my mind to the concept that, perhaps we were not alone.

Putting it to the back of my mind, I carried on my work. I saw Hilary regularly in the health club. She was continuing with bringing in the lights and wished to learn more as now her confidence was restored - she was healed. So, as Merlin says, the easiest way was to show her the ABC.

So one week before Christmas, I climbed another mountain. This site was chosen by Hilary and who was I to refuse. It was wet, cold, extremely cold and snow was on the ground. If I slipped once, I must have slipped a dozen times. This time the mountain was not as steep, but I felt it was a much longer walk, maybe a few miles up. Impressed. Don't be. We have two dogs, one a Labrador called Sam, whose only interest is in food firstly and secondly bitches, especially those on heat. So we got a little bitch, a Heinz 57, from the local pound to keep him out of trouble.

Beauty is a cross between a fox and a collie. That's the only way I can describe her. She has the most enormous ears, which remind you of a fox. Unfortunately, she gets into trouble with other dogs. She is very protective of Sam and guards him jealously, his courting days are over.

Anyway, at the last hurdle, I flagged. I was exhausted. Hilary and Chris were fine. I must get fit. Chris had an idea. Tying the two dogs together and giving me the one lead, they lead me up the last hurdle, through a small wood which was steep and thick in snow.

My trustee huskies must love me, because they pulled me up the last stretch. We were at the top and rewarded by the most beautiful Christmas scene ever. At the top was a small monument, with three sides, indicating three mountain tops and there was three of us. I think today was no accident.

The night before Chris had a strange dream, in which he met John Wayne of all people. John Wayne shook his hand and said in his well known drawl,

'You'll be all right son, you can do it.'

After ten minutes, it took me that long to recover, I directed the other two to the monument. To the right hand side of this monument, was a transmitter/relay station.

We each placed our hand on the one side of the monument and under my guidance, we healed the energy. I asked them after to both close their eyes and relay what they saw. Chris is still skeptic, but was amazed when Hilary related the same pictures as himself. They both saw the energy in white lines opening up all around and then a star. We were not alone. Hilary asked if this energy was anything like the relay station. So I asked her to dowse and use the rods for answers. This she did and got her answer.

This time, the journey back was just as bad as the journey up as the snow had made it treacherous. It was starting to get dark, which made it colder. I was frozen. On returning my mind was thinking why here. Philip said, it was a week before Christmas, what better present for so many small villages but to receive the gift of God's beautiful positive energy. All the churches, the sub-stations would be healed in the area. Wow! and we did that.

'Yes,' said Philip, as I slipped in the snow again.

It's got to be worth it. I must get fit.

After that Hilary got stronger and stronger, going from one coincidence to another. Or are they coincidences? I don't believe they are. Hilary told me that she recognised the work and felt that she had done this work before. It seemed she was remembering colours and what they meant. I knew she didn't need me anymore. In fact, we have kept in touch and I know she will realise her main ambition in life and become a very famous actress one day. At the moment, she has a part in a film starting next year and I feel she will become a household name very soon.

So bless you, Hilary for allowing me to write part of your story, of your path to enlightenment. I know you will help countless others by relaying your story to them. You once said to me, you knew on one occasion, if you picked up the telephone it would change your life and there was no going back. You can see now that you are using the energy, it enables you to see more clearly and become psychically aware. This is God's gift to all who wish to join the Spiritual Pathway in life.

Christmas came. David was now in High School and wanted a computer for Christmas. So he had his wish. I'm still paying for it. However, with the computer came a programme 'Encarta.' This programme was like an encyclopaedia. I enjoyed looking through it.

This year no present from spirit. I was wrong. I said, 'Happy Birthday' to My Lord and enjoyed the day.

Chris and David were playing on the computer - nobody could get a look in until late at night. Merlin was with me and asked if I would like to know who Philip was. Would I! Of course, I would. Merlin sometimes likes games and it was Christmas, so he told me to think about that night I had seen the cross.

The first step, I asked for the name Philip in the Biblical Section. There were loads of them. So, I kept going through each one, until on reading about one Philip, The Apostle, who was nicknamed, 'Philip of the cross.'

Excited, I exclaimed, 'Merlin, I think I've found him.'

Merlin confirmed I was correct. I felt honoured. No wonder, at the beginning, he didn't think me worthy. I felt I wasn't.

That night I was woken up around 2.00 am in the morning..... I saw strange lights and strange shapes, hieroglyphics!!

I was fascinated, totally amazed. When it had finished, I fell asleep and woke up early to Merlin's voice.

'Tonight Jane is special. Meditate in the evening, I will be waiting.'

I carried on through the day as normal wondering what Merlin meant. At 10.00 PM in the evening, I put my favourite music on and brought in the energy, through the colours, sat back and waited.

Merlin was instantly there, in a rush as usual. Also, this time out of breath. He explained, he had been with John most of the day but tonight we were going to Egypt. Meditation, it's like a conscious dream, but very real. Merlin introduced me to an Egyptian who was to be my guide when I journeyed to Egypt in the future. I'm still waiting for that holiday.

We then travelled on to the Great Pyramid and Merlin explained that he had a workshop underneath the pyramid!! This was the reason why I had to learn hieroglyphics.

'So that was you last night, Merlin.' I said out loud.

Merlin explained that the secret of the Great Pyramid has not yet been found. Underneath the Pyramid was just as important. another perfectly shaped pyramid was underneath the one on top. In this pyramid, underneath was a rabbit warren of passages and rooms. Merlin showed me which room has access to the pyramid underneath. He also showed me how to turn the key - the words required in hieroglyphics. In addition, the key was also people, their souls, remember what was discussed earlier, that only those who connected with the place would be able to turn the key. Their energy was the key. Merlin also explained that on this journey to Egypt John would be with me. Well, we haven't gone yet, perhaps, that's another book.

Merlin opened the door and as this has yet to be found, it is best I not write exactly what the door is and where it can be found. We walked down some steps and entered the underneath pyramid. Merlin closed the door and we entered into a passageway which led into many more. We must have walked about half a mile. At each turning, there were more passages and entrances to other rooms.

Merlin opened an old wooden door which led into a large room. Now I have seen some pictures of what Merlin's workshop is suppose to look like, but it is nothing like that. Merlin walked over to a stone slab table. On it were many crystals, all of different colours. These crystals were attached to leather ropes.

'Ahh yes, here it is.' said Merlin and handed me a pale blue crystal.

Although, I say pale blue, I have noticed in the daylight it looks white. There is a definite blue tinge to it.

'This is yours.' said Merlin and he proceeded to place it around my neck. 'When you meditate, Jane, you will see this crystal, in the physical world it is on a lower vibration and you will not be able to see it, but you will be able to feel it.'

Merlin went on to tell me that every spiritual teacher will receive a crystal which represents their colour. However, he did warn me that there has to be balance and where there is light, there is also darkness. Where there is positive, there also has to be negative. Likewise the negative or dark forces will also receive their crystals. Merlin told me he was not looking forward to that job, but it is one God had given him.

I looked around his workshop. It is correct about all sorts of bottles etc but Merlin is very tidy. This was the mind of a very fastidious person who kept everything in tidy order. In one corner there was a large cabinet with small labelled drawers. Job finished, we returned to the top pyramid. I was not allowed to see anymore of the lower pyramid or rather, I think Merlin was in a rush again.

Another time when I was woken up in the middle of the night I was given a sign (See figure one, centre pages)

This sign is called 'The Birth of Light' and whenever I meditate or heal the land the sign comes up in the Tarot. It was not until about six months later that I noticed the sign was practically the same.

This card is represented by three balls of light, white, pink and blue coming up from a central line surrounded in a circle. The meaning of this card is as follows:-

Stay on this path and carry on doing your present activities. Everything is coming into fruition. The Birth of Light is at hand. Realise you are in a state of grace and stay with this feeling. The Birth of Light literally means light created out of the dark. Turning negativity into positive, a product of love.

If you look at the sign, it looks like an upside down peace sign.

Merlin gave me another meaning. At the top of the circle the lines join three times. The middle line is the sun to one side is earth and to the other is heaven. A central beam of light from the three points creates one concentrated beam. This central beam takes away the negativity. In other words, the ABC, it turns negativity into positive by taking away the darkness; a healing mechanism. Think about it.

Anyway back to reality. I have another original sin to eradicate. Merlin tells me it's York and Philip will be with me. Before I go, Merlin tells me to buy an Ordnance Survey map of the area to work out the leys and energy centres before I go.

Here we do again, another trip.

CHAPTER 5

YORK

So early in January I went shopping for an Ordnance Survey map of York. Merlin came with me. In fact, we ended up with two maps. One is the up to date normal Ordnance Survey of York and surrounding areas, the other was York town. The York town map gave the Old Roman and Anglian York. It also showed the modern York.

York remained an important royal and ecclesiastical centre, the seat of a bishop and later, from 735, of an archbishop. Of this great royal and ecclesiastical centre little is yet known archaeologically. Excavations on the Roman fortress walls have shown that they may have survived more or less intact for much of their circuit, and the Anglian tower, a small square tower built to fill a gap in the Roman wall, may be a repair of the Anglian period. The survival of the walls and gates will have meant that the Roman street pattern survived. York was a sophisticated and cosmopolitan place, inhabited by people from all over the Empire.

Much has been written by historians over the years on the importance of York. I'm going further back to knowledge given to me by Merlin which is unknown. York is a spiritual centre, a very important one. So important that thousands of years ago, it was the strongest spiritual centre of Great Britain. It held several stone circles. If you could imagine Stonehenge as the centre and then several larger circles surrounding the ceremonial chamber.

It is the biggest energy centre of Great Britain. Stonehenge was nothing compared to the importance of York. All of this has been destroyed. Merlin told me that the stones used came from all parts of the country, even Ireland. The strength of these stones along with the alignment with other large energy centres, such as Stonehenge, made it a very special place. It might surprise you, that this ceremonial chamber was linked to the pyramids. The reason for these stone circles, I will explain later in the book as it will come as a complete disbelief at this stage. This knowledge is centuries old and a way that our race has forgotten. But nothing is right or wrong, it is all a learning pattern and this race is now ready or will be very soon to understand all the lost knowledge. It has already started.

Back to the maps. I worked out each ley and energy centre on the ordinary Ordnance Survey Map and then turned to the Historical Map.

On working out the energy in York town, I was surprised to find that York Minster was not the centre. York Minster was a 'sub station' but not as strong as an area to the left, roughly about one and a half miles away. On looking at the larger map the leys confirmed this calculation. Another surprise, our ancestors had it right. York Minster's centre of energy was where the ruins of the older, smaller church could be found, which was being excavated. The energy centre of York Minster is slightly to the right of the side entrance and not the main entrance.

So on completing my task on the maps I was ready to go. Merlin stopped me as there was something else I had to do before going. He told me that I would not be on my own and others would come. This surprised me as Chris was not willing to drive there, as it was over a five hour journey. I intended to go alone by train.

'Wait.' said Merlin. Merlin told me that as this was a special task and that York was a large spiritual area, I had to go prepared. Merlin was right . On Sunday, I bought a Sunday paper only to find that the dark forces were using a church in York for occult ceremonies.

'Have faith,' said Merlin. 'You will not be alone.' Merlin stated I would need 'The Creed' on this occasion and therefore needed a Prayer Book. This book is special, Merlin said, because it will guide you all the way. I knew my mother had a Prayer Book and I started to look for it. I couldn't find it. Then one night, I was given a picture in my mind and I saw a book, which was unlike my mother's, the picture also showed me where it was. I flew upstairs and sure enough, I had my Prayer Book,

I don't know where this book came from, I am living in the family house and my father was interested in antiques. This Prayer Book contains the Psalms of David and is for the use of Bishops, Priests and Deacons. I now use it daily.

Merlin states he will not be with me on this journey, but Philip will. I am frightened on what I will encounter, but I know, I am protected and My Lord would not ask me to do this if I was not able.

Sheila knowing I was going to York asked if she could come along with Anne-Marie. I was delighted, Merlin was right. I explained to Sheila that she would probably be bored as I intended to visit many churches and also Roman remains. It was not a shopping trip. I was thinking of Anne-Marie, who was now a teenager, and the lore of the clothes shops may be too great. But no, I was delighted when Sheila said it doesn't matter they would love to come.

So armed with maps, prayer book and sandwiches we embarked the train. I felt all I needed was the bell and candles, this phrase had been going through my mind for some time; bell, book and candles. I now have the book and candles and I'm just waiting for the bell.

I cannot have been much company for Sheila and Anne-Marie as most of the journey I was doing my prayer work and as the train turned northwards, I started opening up the leys and energy centres on the way. I saw in my mind a corridor of light as the train trundled northward. Philip asked me to keep going, I was nearly there.

'York?' I enquired, as I knew we had a way to go yet.

'No, just keep going, Jane, you'll see.'

In my mind I could see the light spreading, beautiful. The energy was surging through my feet and as the energy opened, I felt euphoria again. I love my spiritual work. I was in heaven. On nearing York, I had the most wonderful experience, how can I put it into words.

Philip explained afterwards that I had to be pure to open York. It was such a strong spiritual area that only a pure person could have opened it up. What I felt on the train was eradication of my last sin. I had balanced my Karma. I knew this only afterwards. But on that train I felt the purple cloak of Christ surround my physical body. I closed my eyes and saw it and then Oh! joy, My Master's voice. 'You now learn from The Father.'

It was only then did I realise that My Lord had always been with me and had never left my side. We all might have guides, but The Lord is with all of us. I no longer feared anything, not even cleaning York. Philip explained that this was a special event but on returning home, I would have to face my greatest fear on my own and overcome it. On balancing your Karma everybody has to face their greatest fear, it is the last test.

We disembarked from the train and made our way through York town to the Minster. On the way there was a small church, I entered with Anne-Marie, who was curious about the work I was doing. I knelt and said The Lord's Prayer and then prayed to God that with his beautiful white light to release the spirits trapped. There were no trapped spirits. Strange. Philip told me that they knew I was coming and that all the spirits had congregated in the Minster. Apparently, they had been there for days, more arriving each day. Philip also told me that only in one or two areas would I find further spirits.

I didn't need to look at the map on entering The Minster, I knew exactly where I was going. This was a tourist area and a lot of people were milling around, but I didn't care, I was doing My Father's work. So quite close to the side entrance, which was crowded with people, I discreetly stepped on a marble slab. The centre of the energy. So kind of the church to place a marble slab there, curious the Minster's floor is stone. I wonder if the church know this knowledge?

After finishing my prayer work, I felt quite dizzy and as I sat out of the way in a side seat, I saw a dishevelled face. It was a monk but this face was not at all peaceful. I felt I knew this person and had worked with him before. I felt it was my fault he had suffered. I prayed for forgiveness and was rewarded by seeing a more peaceful and loving monk's face. The surge of energy was terrific.

This large spiritual church needed healing and the spirits, Oh! so many of them waiting. I can't believe that our priests, our ministers have not done their work. It made me very sad, something was very seriously lacking. This Minster had also been struck by lightening. God indeed was angry with this place. I left, I had more work to do.

We noticed a craft fair in the adjoining buildings to the Minster and decided to look around. As we went upstairs to the craft room the energy hit the place. Wow! I can never get used to that feeling. I was in heaven, a permanent smile on my face. It was like that wherever I went as each church opened up.

I was getting tired, all this running around. I had asked Sheila and Anne-Marie if they were all right as we must have walked miles. Sheila suggested something to eat. I must get fit.

I made notes of this journey so I could remember every detail. The city was healed at 4.30 p.m. in the afternoon. One stray soul I found on the city walls, another on a flight of stairs in one of the towers. At 5.30 p.m. the souls were still going to the light in the Minster. That should give you some idea as to how many were waiting. In fact, Philip told me that some had been waiting for a century or more.

I was exhausted, mentally and physically. This work does make me tired as the negativity as you heal goes through you, just like a channel. You are healing the energy by channelling the negativity through yourself. Well, I did ask My Father to make me a vessel of His Peace, so I mustn't complain.

One thing I didn't find was a pink house. I had seen psychically a pink house which I knew was important. Nevermind, I'll come back another day. Today, we didn't have time to look.

Returning home on the train I said a prayer of thanks. I saw that the souls were still going towards the light.

The next day I felt awful. So much negativity has effected me and made me ill. I still feel tired and sick. Philip told me that there was a celebration for the work done and spirit would help take out the negativity for me, helping to restore the balance. Apparently, lots of spirits wish to help. I am gladdened by the news, but it didn't make my stomach feel any better.

I felt the need for confirmation of the healing of York, so I went to spiritualist church. I wonder if they will pick up on the work I am doing. Merlin thought this was a good idea, in fact, he said he would speak to the medium.

Merlin was as good as his word. The medium picked on me and asked if I had recently had some writing published. I said, yes, as this was the article on the ley and energy centres around Cardiff.

The medium told me in a strange voice. 'You think nobody is listening to you, Ahh shame,' she paused, 'but they are.'

I nearly laughed, she had Merlin's voice off to a tee. His sense of humour came through as well. She went on.

'Ahh shame nobody is listening to the poor girl. Well, you are wrong, they are listening. I see a bookcase behind you. All the books on the middle shelf are your own work.'

I was surprised, Merlin never told me that one. Me write a book, well only with spirits help.

I enjoyed the service so much, I decided to go back the following week. This time I met a very open minded couple who I was able to read so easily. May and Philip I saw regularly to talk to in church and we made friends. In fact, it was some surprise to find out that Chris had worked with Philip in the past. To avoid any confusion, I think I will call May's hubby, Phil.

Phil was not a well man, he had suffered with a failing kidney and was on the transplant list at the local hospital. He recently attended church for spiritual healing and found it a great comfort.

That night, I meditated.

Philip and Mary were there and wanted to take me to a meeting. In a large airy room was an enormous glass oval table with twelve seats. There were lots of windows to the room and I saw darkness and in the darkness were stars. At the top of the table sat, well I can never get her/his name right, but I call her KH. KH is the organiser of the lights. Also, KH has no gender. Sometimes, I see the female and other times, when KH is serious, I see the male. Most times I see her as a female, so to avoid any confusion I will refer to KH as a female.

She is dressed in a long white robe which has a cape attached. Inside the cape is a sparkling, white material, something I have never seen on this earth. The strangest thing of all is her hat, it looks like a white Dutch cap.

KH invites me to sit down. Someone is standing next to me and offers me a seat. It is My Lord. I fall on my knees and look into his eyes. He is beautiful. I feel at peace. This is reward enough for all the work I have done on His behalf and here He is offering me a seat. KH asks me again to sit down and I get up with His assistance and sat down.

KH explains that there is more work to do. The earth is in a precarious position and again she gives me the sign of The Birth of Light. I look into her eyes and I see a galaxy, no time, no it is unexplainable, it's everything. I see worlds, space, wisdom and knowledge. I felt dizzy and thought the best thing was to come out of the meditation. Immediately Merlin was at my side and accompanied as well by Mary and Philip, I returned.

That night, I was woken up at 2.00 am in the morning, another sign. This time, it was a circle with two doves in it. The doves held twigs in their beaks. I remember John telling me of this sign as well. I knew I had to search for a stained glass window. Oh well, more travelling.

In the morning, Merlin was there. He was telling me to bring in another colour, yellow. He explained that this was enlightenment and would open up the crown. I didn't really understand what he meant and I didn't have a chance to ask questions as he was gone again - off on his travels always in a rush.

I've realised, I have never explained what Merlin looks like. Well, if you have ever seen Walt Disney's version of 'Sword in the Stone' you would have a picture which to everybody is Merlin.

Let me enlighten you. Merlin is tall, very tall and has hardly any hair on his head except for a grey ring around by his ears, just like a monk. The reason why I know this is because he doesn't ever wear a hat. I have never seen him in any kind of head gear. He wears a long gown with a cape which I have seen in blue and purple. The colour could even be a mixture of the two. The cape has a very large, high collar which totally surrounds his face.

His eyes are the bluest you have ever seen and they twinkle when he is in his mischievous mood. In all, he has a gentle kind face but does give an air of authority. Indeed, he strikes an impressive pose, one never to be forgotten.

I brought in the yellow light and did feel a tingle on my crown. I didn't find out what that actually meant until later.

That night, I was tired and went to bed early. Chris stayed up to watch something on the television. I couldn't settle, I felt restless. I closed my eyes - THERE WAS THE DEVIL. I have never been attacked like this. Do I scream. Do I call for help. Do I panic - OH YES - I panicked. My heart was beating very, very fast. I opened my eyes he was still there, I could feel his presence. He had actually blocked off my escape from the bedroom. Think fast. Was I going to hell. No I had forgotten, you face your darkest fear on your own and how you overcome that fear was the way you learn the last step to enlightenment.

I'm sorry, but He will not allow me to tell you that last step as you have to learn that one yourself. All I can say is that it was not easy. But I am allowed to give you some help and that is to remember Our Lord's words and the teachings on the way to that ultimate test of faith.

I was rewarded for overcoming my fear. Don't get me wrong, I still know when the devil is around. My crown opened and now I know when I receive messages. There are two messengers from heaven. One are angels and the other direct. If you are enlightened you will know the difference. I now also feel spirit messages through the crown. I have proved this over and over again with the cards. In fact, now I am glad to see the message card when I am stuck, I know I'm going to get help. At this very moment I am receiving messages through the crown as this has been a very difficult part to write and I needed help.

John telephoned.

He explained that due to work on the farm he had delayed going to Ireland but he intended to go next weekend, could he stay. Of course. I looked forward to seeing him.

John arrived with Nathan and Gary. John and I caught up to date with each other's activities and he decided to visit Cardiff Castle. He was interested in the room in the clock tower. He agreed with me that the Bute family certainly understood some of the knowledge and had used it to some extent.

I took to Gary straight away. John and Gary usually worked together. Gary was more interested in ley alignment and the position of the stars and their constellations in respect of the earth energy. His knowledge on the old sites is quite formidable. I felt I had known him before.

Well, what can I say about Nathan. It was Nathan they had gone to Ireland to bring back, along with his belongings. Nathan was not a young man and I saw straight away he was not well. Nathan looked at me and said to my surprise.

'Ah a crown shakra.'

'Shakra? What is a shakra.' I replied.

'You are open to crown messages.' Nathan went on. 'Will you give me a reading and a healing?'

I love my work. I love giving healings and to see people appreciate God's strength through these healings. Nathan is quite a character and in his cards I saw he was enlightened. Although John is psychic himself, he is not quite as strong in seeing and asked if I would have a look at a certain area, on an Ordnance Survey map, to see if I could pick up anything.

I placed my hand on the area and immediately pictures formed. I could see a small hill with ridges all the way to a flat top. Then a maze cut out of turf. This small mound was in a field surrounded by trees with a path going partly around the outside of the field. To one side, at the bottom, there was a copse. I felt this was where John had to go next. In fact, much later, John confirmed that everything I had seen was correct and it had helped him find the place.

That afternoon, Dave came down and we all went to Cardiff Castle. Gary commented on the fact that the city felt wonderful. The energy was truly healed. I love being with like minds, it confirms everything that I do. Halfway through the tour of the castle, Nathan disappeared. We found him outside, he felt the decadence of the castle overwhelming and had to leave. He is right, it is a truly decadent place full of gold leaf and splendour.

Nathan lives very simply, doing his spiritual work mainly out of doors. He was truly one with nature. All too quickly they had to leave and I was sorry to see them go.

I felt my crown open and a kiss. 'Ahh! Merlin, I love you.' I said to an empty room. Merlin was back to explain what a shakra was. Apparently, there are points on your body which can open up to feeling and seeing. On the palms of your hands are two round circles, these are the palm shakras. Merlin went on to explain all the points of the body and what their purpose was. On the forehead, another shakra, this one helped with clairvoyance, the third eye. Merlin explained that the crown shakra was the last to open and I was truly, in Indian words, a shaman.

PICTURE ONE
Bulls at the end of the gate to the field where the windmill is located. The trees shown is the energy centre.

PICTURE TWO
The Old Windmill

PICTURE THREE
Circle of stones in ground of Cardiff Castle.

PICTURE FOUR
Cardiff Castle.

PICTURE FIVE
David and his friends camping at Castle Morgraig.

PICTURE SIX
Castle Coch.

FIGURE ONE
Birth of Light.

FIGURE TWO
The Cerne Abbas Giant.

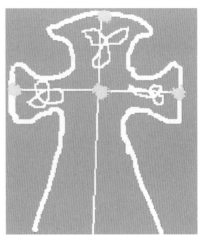

FIGURE THREE
Birth of Light.
(The key to the wheel)

FIGURE FOUR
The Celtic Cross
(The Birth of Light sign)

FIGURE FIVE
'The Wheel' shown in meditation.

FIGURE SIX
The Celtic Cross (Wheel)

FIGURE SEVEN

FIGURE EIGHT

PYRAMID PROTECTION

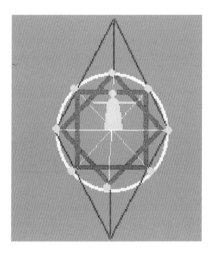

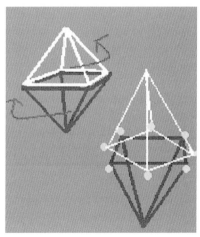

FIGURE NINE
(The wheel/celtic cross)

FIGURE TEN
Procedure

CHAPTER SIX

The Teacher

Imeditated. Mary and Philip were there, but no Merlin. Mary and Philip took me to the church, the white cathedral which was carved out of a rock face. As we walked up the long, steep path I saw angels gathering around us. As the doors of the Cathedral were closed Philip knocked and indicated I should enter. Wow! trumpets sound as if someone important had arrived. I turned round to see who it was only to be ushered in by Mary. It was for me!! I walked up the isle, halfway up was my mother and her sister Muriel dressed in sacking. What was going on.

I knew I couldn't stop because KH was at the top waiting, so I smiled at my relatives and walked on. I arrived before KH and My Lord. I knelt. I felt this was a very solemn and holy occasion. KH drew a sword of light. She was bringing the sword down through me, I felt it.

My Lord said. 'Arise, you have now been ordained as a Leader of the Spirit, My Minister. Remember, you have been ordained by your Lord, conduct yourself accordingly, as you will be judged more harshly that those you will teach.' I was overcome with emotion. Was this real.

KH helped me up, my legs were wobbly. Merlin was at my side and helped me out of the cathedral. I stopped to look at my mother, her face was a picture. The pride I could see in her eyes.

Merlin brought me back and whispered to me, 'Act like a Guardian, you now have the power.'

'A Guardian, Merlin?'

Merlin explained, that I was now a Guardian of the Light.

Did it really happen? As always, I return to prayer. I looked in my special Prayer Book and randomly opened the book to any page. There staring out from the page was the Prayer for ordination of priests.

Back to reality. I have my sign, remember, the two doves in a circle. Chris and I must have visited all the churches in Cardiff and surrounding areas, but there was no stained glass window with that design. I think we have to go further afield. As a lot of weekends were taken up with this task, I had by now given up. A rest from the work would be a good idea as sometimes, when you are not looking, it all comes together.

Chris suggested going to Tintern Abbey. This abbey was located in a very pretty part of the country and I could relax as there are no stained glass windows as it was a ruin.

Tintern Abbey

The abbey was founded in 1131 by Cistercian monks, an order that farmed on a large scale. The picturesque ruins beside the Wye date mainly from the 13th century. The abbey was dissolved in 1536. The main structure is still standing and the inside of the main church is now grassed with seats in it. I sat on one of the seats and like always wherever I am I do my work. After saying the Lord's Prayer, I prayed for God's beautiful white light to heal the energy and for any spirits trapped to go to the white light.

Suddenly, I saw a monks face smiling at me. This monk suddenly sprouted wings and waving was gone. I thought nothing more of it. Like all tourists we walked around the abbey and then visited the gift shop. I bought a beautiful CD, called appropriately, 'A Crown of Light.' This contained choral and organ music from The Cathedral and Abbey Church of St. Alban. It contains the Lord's Prayer and The Creed. In fact, I now meditate to this CD, it is very special music to me.

I was drawn to one of the tourist gift shops on the end of a block of shops. This pink coloured shop had many windows displaying all types of tourist gifts. Outside, was a rack of tee-shirts. I was strangely drawn to these tee-shirts and the very first rack, the top shirt had an emblem on the front. You guessed it, a circle with two doves inside holding twigs in their mouths and yes, this was the pink house I had been looking for. That's how it happens. I was guided to the right place at the right time to do My Father's work. I looked across at the ruins of the abbey. Of course, I am stupid, there is a round window right at the top of the church. The stained glass long gone.

On the return journey, I smiled, contented, I had completed the assignment.

Next day, Merlin told me, I was to become a guide for those who sought me out, or as he put it sent by spirit. Merlin was going to show me a way to heal via a map. I needed an atlas. So I searched our bookshelves and found an old one. Next, he said I would need the Ordnance Survey map of South Wales. This was easy, I had used an Ordinance Survey map when I healed the area, remember, marking out the leys and energy centres. Next, he said, a crystal.

'What type of crystal, Merlin?' I enquired. Immediately, a picture came into my mind of an old necklace I had as a teenager, a crystal. The chain had long gone, but the crystal remained in my jewellery box. I went and retrieved it.

'What next, Merlin?'

'That's it.' came the reply.

Merlin showed me that by putting the crystal on a thread and by using the energy, in the form of bringing in the colours, you actually heal by the map. On this occasion, the colour was orange. First Merlin said bring in the white, pink and blue as normal and then orange.

By holding the crystal over the map, I was amazed to see it move. If an area is healed, the crystal goes round in circles. If the area was negative, the crystal went up and down showing the direction of the ley line across the map. Amazing and so simple, anyone could do it.

The healing takes the same form as on the land. By placing your hand on the area that needed healing you say The Lord's Prayer. Then, with God's beautiful white light, heal the leys and energy and then asking trapped spirits to go towards the white light, not to be afraid, they will be with their loved ones, their family and friends, Amen. Without lifting your hand from the map, push down the orange light through the palm shakra.

This, Merlin explained, is what you will teach. I admit that I was a bit skeptic, but spirit have not sent anyone to me yet that couldn't pick up that energy. I teach my pupils to dowse, to crystal dowse, eradication of their original sin and where to go to eradicate it. Of course, each and every one has had to do a healing on the map first. All have been able to dowse and confirm to themselves on what they are doing. Some are more open that others. I have had one person experience the second world war on her healing and believe me she was much too young. Some cry, others feel nothing, but still get confirmation of the healing via the crystal. It works, come and see for yourself.

Merlin states that this should be able to give me a living in the future, as I dearly wish to do my spiritual work full-time.

Back to the map of South Wales. In the morning I completed the whole map. This work made me very tired. Before, I was just healing a city or a small area. I slept all afternoon. It was Saturday, I wanted to go to church.

Chris drives me down to the church but very rarely attends - he is still skeptic but still helps. Bless those who believe without seeing or feeling, for their faith is strong.

On the way down I asked Merlin if he was going to help give a message about what I have just done because, as always, I seek confirmation that I am doing My Father's work. I still watch out for that old devil.

We very rarely get a man as the medium, so it was with some surprise that he picked on me.

'Do you realise' he said ' who is standing next to you. She is a very religious lady.'

I thought of Mary. ' Yes' I replied.

He went on. 'Do you really realise who is standing next to you.'

'Of course.' I said I could see him shake his head in disbelief and I smiled. He asked again if I really knew, smiling, I replied again, that I knew. Then he stated he had a gentleman too, standing by the other side of me.

'He works with bones,' the medium went on.

I was puzzled - bones?

The medium corrected himself, 'runes, cards - he's a magician!!' He exclaimed.

Well did I really need much more proof if other mediums can see them. Again, he asked if I knew who it was and I replied yes. Twice more he asked did I know who it was. By this time I could feel the attention of many eyes on me.

'I smiled at the medium. 'Of course I know who it is, do you really want me to say.'

The medium looked embarrassed. He went on. 'You are enlightened and working up and down the levels. The magician is teaching you everything he knows. The medium couldn't retain his curiosity any longer, looking me straight in the eyes he said. 'What are you doing, will you teach us what you are doing?'

I smiled and replied. 'I'm doing lots of things.'

The medium immediately started speaking again. 'Spirit thanks you for all the work that you have done and request please do not stop.' Oh! Merlin, I got my confirmation and no, I love you too much to stop. Thank you Mary for being there and proving to me that my work is valuable, I love you.

After the service, May and Phil stopped me to talk. They asked if they could come up to the house to learn more. Of course, I would look forward to it.

It was now early January and Chris' 40th Birthday. I wanted to get him something special, something he always wanted, to give him an interest, as you can tell by now with working full time and my spiritual work I was kept pretty busy. People calling at the house all the time to see me, he felt a bit left out. So one weekend, we went shopping in town.

I had a message. Oh! this is very materialistic, was I listening to the right source, is that old devil back? We went into a well known electrical store and I think for the first time in Chris' life I surprised him. I asked an assistant to show us a video camera. Something I knew Chris would love, he deserved it. The assistant picked out a very simple model and might I add, one of the most expensive and proceeded to show us how it worked. Chris looked at me his face puzzled. Out of my mouth came words I could not believe I had said them, I was not alone.

'What is that one there.' I said pointing to a smaller model but of the same make.

'Ah, good taste.' said the assistant. Apparently, this one was even more expensive, it would be, but it did absolutely everything you could think of.

I asked in my mind if this was OK, surely it was materialistic. No reply. They were not going to help as I have learnt we still have free will.

I made a decision. 'All right, we'll have it, thank you.'

Chris' face was a picture. Although, I have told him it was not only his 40th Birthday present but also his Christmas present, his following Birthday present etc.

Chris could not hide his delight. I know him. He would never in a million years have asked for himself. So now and then, you know what men are like they have to have a new toy. Little did I know spirit had planned this and he would use his new toy for spiritual purposes and enjoy it.

I love Chris, he has stood by me all these years having to put up with a cause he doesn't believe in - or does he?

Merlin direct me to a map in the house, one belonging to my father whose hobby I might add, was collecting maps. I was very fortunate as a lot of the maps required I already had except for the two for York.

This time the whole of Wales was to be healed on Sunday morning. The healing was filmed by Chris. Without any rehearsal it was taped. Chris has actually managed to put my symbol on the front and back of this film. My symbol is the Celtic Cross. A simple cross in purple with silver/turquoise on the outside. Guess who picked it? - no prizes for the winner of the correct answer.

That tape I now use in helping to teach.

I meditated. I love meditating, I see all my friends, Mary, Philip, Merlin, KH, My Lord. The others around that table I have not, as yet, met. There are twelve seats and Philip explained that there were twelve lights on the Council. I was surprised to note that only nine members were present at any one time. Out of all my friends, only Merlin and My Lord were members of this Council. KH was like an organiser of the lights. Mary and Philip never sat at that table and as for the others, I don't know them, they were just a blur. I think I was not, at this stage, allowed to see them.

Philip also explained that the Council members in turn organised the angels and archangels. KH welcomed me and holding my hand took me out of the room onto a balcony. This balcony overlooked a beautiful, what I could describe as a park, a rather large park with a small lake, a stream coming out of the lake and a waterfall. Angels were walking, talking, sitting just like everyday activity. I can never get used to looking at an angel - they are beautiful.

Mary and Philip then took me to the cathedral in the cliff. Crowds had gathered, including angels. I felt they were celebrating. I looked at myself, I was dressed in a long flowing white gown with a cape attached. On my head, I felt a band of gold. Around my waist gold braid was tied. In the cathedral, Oh! great joy, my mother and my aunt were there and presented to me. This time I could hug and kiss them. What a celebration. I stood back and looked at my mum, her eyes shining with pride, she was still dressed in sacking. I thought of what Merlin had told me about now having the power, I was a Guardian of the Light and to act accordingly.

I stood back and thought she should be an angel, as she was in her physical lifetime. Instantly, my mum was an angel. Wow! this is good. My aunt can she be an angel too? - it worked. My mum was crying looking at herself. We just hugged and hugged the three of us. Oh no! here come the tears. It was such an emotional scene.

Now, if ever I call Merlin, or I am distressed, I see Merlin coming with two angels, my mum and my aunt. What a beautiful sight.

I telephoned John about Tintern Abbey. He was pleased and told me a very similar story. Apparently, he had to find a place which was on the Ordnance Survey map but he couldn't find it on the land. He had tried several times to find the right place, to no avail. One weekend, he went down a lane and stopped his car at the bottom. A lonely church stood with a small graveyard and next to it the vicarage. A large dog wandered over to him as he got out of the car. This dog made a fuss of him and kept looking over to where a path was. John got the message and followed him. In fact, John followed him for over a mile through woodland. Wondering whether this was a wild goose chase he came across a very old monument and an even older tree. John instantly knew this was the place.

The dog strangely enough went up to the tree and sat down. John proceeded to do his work of healing and when he had finished the dog got up and directed him back to the car. Again the dog made a fuss of him and stayed long enough for John to take a photograph of him. Then with a wag of the tail, he was gone. That reminds me. I must ask John for a copy of that photograph as I would like to include it in this book.

So pay attention to nature, signs and people, they are all doing God's work in helping you along the spiritual path to enlightenment.

Dave telephoned.

'Can I come down, I've got something for you.' I'm always delighted to see Dave. The two families have known each other since the children were born.

The weather was getting warmer and we were sitting outside on the patio when he arrived. He was carrying a large plastic bag which was full of books. You know the type of bag I mean, one of those large bin bags. The books were religious books, all ages, all types, except one. It was a fairly modern 'Let's Go' book for a young person, full of ideas about careers, colleges etc.

We talked for a while and Dave asked if I was interested in attending another paranormal conference in Cardiff. I decided to go.

Chris, who now had his camera, decided he too would like to attend but not for the two days. Chris thought it would be a good idea to film some of the speakers, that is, if it was an interesting topic. Little did I know that one of the speakers would be me!!

I brought the bag of books into the hall and wondered out loud, 'well Father, why have I got these?' The spiritual path never ceases to amaze me.

'Line them up on the sideboard,' a gentle voice answered, one I had never heard before. I obeyed. The sideboard was now full of religious books, Oh except that one. 'What next.' I said to an empty room.

I felt it before I heard it. I felt overwhelming love. I closed my eyes to see but there was nothing to see. I tingled all over, it felt a bit like York all over again. The room vibrated and I heard a voice.

'Each and every book has a name in it. Each pupil you teach, ask them to choose their book by touch. Each person has been carefully chosen. They will know their book.'

My Father, I love you. I felt very honoured.

It's true. One girl I saw that her karma in a past life was connected with cruelty to animals. You guessed it, she chose the only non religious book. She opened up the book and there on the page was volunteers for the RSPCA, The Royal Society for Protection of Cruelty to Animals. There have been many cases of coincidences like that with these books. But there again, I don't believe in coincidences anymore.

The books on the sideboard are going down much to my relief. However, Dave telephoned again.

'I don't know why I'm doing this Jane, but I'm still collecting religious books for you. I should have another bag full soon.'

Well Father, keep sending them and I'll keep teaching them. I love you.

John telephoned. Could he stay. He wished to attend the conference. He was coming alone.

The weekend of the conference arrived. I love being with like minds. It's the people you meet. Merlin told me to take my cards, map and crystal. I would obviously need them to help teach. Merlin was with Mary. 'No Jane, this time you must talk. You have to talk, your words are not just for the individuals.' I am not really happy about this as I am not too confident about talking in public. I have noticed that when I ask My Father for strength and courage I feel my crown opening up and in comes strength.

One of the speakers did not turn up, so it was decided that they would hold a workshop in which members of the conference could talk. John and Dave smiled at me. It was like an unspoken word. Oh No! I'm not talking to hundreds of people. Dave and John looked at each other and smiled. What do they know that I don't. Oh No! No!

During the day I met many people. Some approached for a reading and others to learn. One woman was a leader in a Spiritualist Church. I taught her to bring in the three main colours, white, pink and blue. I healed and asked her to pick up a further colour. On holding her hands I pushed into her the colour orange. I was delighted when she confirmed the colour. Strange, on putting in the orange colour through her body I could see muddy areas and some black.

Merlin explained that the muddy areas were usually emotional problems, which if not healed, could lead to physical problems. The black area was a physical problem which needed attention. Merlin, I love you, don't ever stop teaching me. The woman was able to dowse after picking up the energy and proceeded to heal an area on the map. I explained to her that she had two karmas. One was in Cardiff castle, she broke her husband's heart by running off with a handsome knight in armour. 'Funny,' she said, 'I always have problems with my love life, I always think the grass is greener with someone else.'

As she herself was psychic, she told me there was a very tall man watching us. He was very interested in the crystal dowsing and was leaning over the map as the healing took place. She went on describing this man. 'He's wearing a long blue cape with a very high collar.' I started to laugh. 'You know him,' she said questioning. 'Oh vaguely,' I replied.

Another woman approached and asked would I mind healing her brother. She too had watched the healing and overheard that the orange light could heal from a distance. I asked her if she had a photograph of her brother. Yes, at home. She was to fetch the photograph the following day.

I explained about God's light through colours and asked her to try it. This knowledge is for everyone. She thanked me and would see me the following day.

That is how most of the day went. I think, I actually only heard one speaker as most of the time I was out in the garden, which was attached to the conference hall, talking to people and teaching.

The workshop was to be held in the evening, so we all came back to my house for tea. Chris decided he would attend the workshop bringing his camera with him.

The hall was still crowded and a middle aged man got up on the stage. He related an experience his family went through when travelling down to Devon for a family holiday. As the children were anxious to arrive at their destination they left very early in the morning. Suddenly, they saw lights in the sky and their vehicle mysteriously stopped. Apparently, they had missing time and the whole incident had changed them. He explained, that he no longer worried about his job or materialism. His hobby, photography, had taken over his life. He was more concerned about conservation.

I was not paying my whole attention to his talk until he mentioned that he and his family now looked forward to climbing mountains. He was also taking an interest in earth energy and he didn't know why. I had taken a copy of my article about leys and energy centres and decided to talk to him when he was finished.

However, I didn't get a chance to see him that day as a young woman got up on the stage and related her experiences. I was strangely drawn to her, I just felt I knew her. All the time I was being pushed by Merlin and Philip down to the rostrum and it was the reason why I didn't pay too much attention to what the first speaker was saying.

No way did I want to talk at this conference. Merlin was trying to persuade me. For every step forwards, I was fighting two back. No way Merlin.

This young woman was telling her story of seeing lights in the sky. She related strange dreams where she was told the secrets of the pyramids. She went further into those secrets and I was the only one in the audience who knew she was telling the truth.

This young woman was very nervous, but explained, she was being pushed onto the rostrum to tell her story. That was it. That's all I needed. OK Merlin, give me the strength to do this. Chris had disappeared, I think he was out in the garden when I went onto the rostrum. I started to speak about the energy, about healing. I confirmed what the previous speaker was talking about. Better still, I taught that audience to bring in God's light and asked if anybody tingled.

To my amazement half the audience put up their hands. When I came off the stage the young woman and I looked at each other. I went over to where she was sitting. She just rose from her chair and we hugged. Two lost souls coming together. We went outside and talked.

Her name was Helen and she had travelled from Devon to this conference. Not really understanding why it was so important to attend. She was also amazed to find herself on the stage talking. I could see she was on the spiritual pathway herself and one of her original sins was Cardiff.

Not knowing anyone in Cardiff she was to stay with a friend of one of the organisers that night and intended to return to Devon Sunday night. Merlin was guiding me, this girl needed help with her original sin.

'Would you like to stay at my house tomorrow night and then you can travel back to Devon Monday morning.' I told her to think about it and to see me tomorrow in the conference.

On arriving back in the hall, nearly everybody had left. Chris was with the others packing up his camera. He looked at me and smiled shaking his head.

Apparently, he had let the camera run through the talks and not knowing I was going to speak, well how could he, the battery had run out half way through my talk. He looked sheepishly. 'Sorry kidda.' That's his nickname for me. I didn't mind one little bit, I didn't think I did all that well.

We all went back to the house. Both John and Dave knew I would talk today. One thing I have learnt, you can see for everybody else but when it comes to yourself you don't. Some things I see but very rarely. John had decided he was leaving Sunday night to return to Dorset.

The following day, I was approached by several people, all of whom had heard my talk. One man approached and asked if I could teach him. His name was Paul and he was fascinated with the subject of karma. I looked at him and said. 'You should be in Caerleon in Newport for eradication of one of your original sins.'

His mouth dropped open and he couldn't hide his look of surprise. 'I live in Caerleon Road in Newport.' he replied.

I asked him if he wished to come back to my house later on in the afternoon, after the conference, to learn more. He was delighted. I left Chris talking to Paul as I was interrupted by a lady holding a photograph. I felt the photograph before looking at the picture, it was already warm. This was the lady whose brother was ill. I brought in the orange light and proceeded with the healing. The lady kissed my cheek and said thank you, the photograph was now hot.

She went on to explain that she had brought in the lights last night, just as I had taught her. She felt coldness down her legs. Her legs were giving her trouble and she walked with a stick. As I have already explained, this knowledge is for all of us, I am just the teacher. We all have the ability to heal ourselves through God's love and energy.

Helen approached me. She would be delighted to take up my offer and stay the night. I was looking forward to her company, I felt we had much to discuss. I could see that in the future she would be a spiritual teacher, but not in this country.

Earlier in the year Merlin had directed me to a book on the bottom shelf in a book store. This book was half hidden as it was so small. It told the story of Atlantis. I knew this book was special but it was not for me. I read the book briefly, it was all very familiar. I think this book is for Helen, I'm not sure until I talk to her.

Chris attended this day at the conference. He was enjoying filming different people and certain parts of the talks which he found interesting.

I managed to speak to the man who gave the first talk in the workshop and gave him my article. He felt he was connected to Helen and had given her one of his photographs. Oh! what a beautiful picture. It was of a statue of an angel by the sea. He had caught the image perfectly at a moment when a beam of light hit the angel's head. It was stunning.

However, a nagging doubt was crossing my mind. This family were only drawn on the spiritual pathway after seeing lights in the sky and what he relayed was missing time. I put it to the back of my mind for the time being. What I didn't know was that I would remember this occasion in the future.

Everybody came back to the house, including Helen. Paul explained that he would return later as he had promised to give a lift home to a friend he had brought to the conference.

After tea, John and Dave left. I was sorry to see John go but I knew he had a long drive in front of him. Paul arrived. So Helen, Paul, Chris and I sat out on the patio and talked. I got out my maps to teach

Paul. Helen watched but did not participate. Paul was surprised to find he could dowse and pick up the energy quite easily.

He healed an area on the map. Helen picked up the dowsing rods. Immediately, she started dowsing. We all stayed up until gone 1.00 AM in the morning. I thoroughly enjoyed their company.

Paul had decided to buy his own dowsing rods and to eradicate the original sin in Caerleon and asked if I would help on the first one. Of course I would. He took my telephone number and told me he would be in touch.

After Paul had gone, Chris went to bed and Helen and I talked. I gave her the book, as by now she was getting interested in Atlantis. Oh Merlin, you are never wrong. We finally turned in around 3.00 AM in the morning.

We were all tired but Helen wanted to leave early. So around 10.00 AM I walked her to the bus stop to see her safely on her way.

We both got upset and hugged each other. She told me that there was something for me in the bedroom. I knew that although we might talk by telephone, I would never see her again. I was sad, she was a beautiful person.

Helen had left a letter for me and I hope she will not mind but I wish to put it in this book. The letter reads:-

'Dear Jane,

Waking up, I'm full of thoughts - things I would like to say and I don't know if we'll have the time together for me to cover.

You have a gift and I think you can trust to using it wisely and well. At least, I can feel that something quite deep has happened to me from this weekend.

The power of the ego, especially on a spiritual level, is the greatest danger you will have to face. We cannot love or hate anything about others, unless it reflects something we love or hate about ourselves. Do you know who I am talking about? me, of course. Well, that's the ego for you - tricky little critters at the best of times.

Because for one reason or another there is a kind of bond between us, if I ever feel that you are in danger and Chris or David are not already there to protect you, I will come to you. See how well protected you can be! That's part of your gift and just as well you have such innocence.

When your book is published in three or four years, I'll come to buy one of the first copies. In the meantime, your emblem will help you, put it by your donations cup and use it as your logo. Don't be afraid to ask to have your needs met; you know you would do everything in your power to provide for those who asked of you. Learning the other side of the coin doesn't automatically necessitate to becoming a materialist, as you fear. Yes, I know you do! But you won't if you keep a constant vigil for the ego, your own and others.

Now it's time to put the metaphysical soap box away - it's definitely taken up it's space. See, I feel compelled to do my thing too and I know I'm not always on the right track, cos the damn thing makes such scraping noises sometimes, as I drag it around with me, but I hope on this occasion it didn't cause too much disquiet to your ears. Your hospitality was beautiful and I will really treasure the book, I'm aware how special it is.

God Bless, Helen'

Oh! Darling Helen. I mirror people. The spiritual ego is yours, my poor darling.

One of the reasons, Merlin had explained, why I was so much persecuted in this lifetime, was a gift. A gift, more like a curse. I mirror people, they see in me what they don't like about themselves. Helen had seen it.

The next day she telephoned and told me her story of her eradication of one sin, of all places, in Cardiff bus station.

Her bus wasn't going to arrive for one hour. As she sat on a bench she recalled the events of the weekend. Suddenly, as a conscious dream or a vision, she saw what had happened in a past life.

In this lifetime, again, she was a spiritual teacher, a leader of a group of people. She told them, that if she could, she would come back to prove to them, that there is life after death. On dying, she wanted them to know that she was still with them, but in spirit. So when she died she was determined to do just that. In a service which her group attended she dematerialised as an angel. On doing this she acquired an original sin for spiritual ego.

Once she realised what she had done, Helen asked Our Lord for forgiveness. Immediately, she was covered in an orange glow. She knew she was forgiven.

On coming out of this trance the people on the bus stop had changed and were smiling at her. People were now asking her to look after their baggage, stopping to talk or smiling to her as they passed by.

Darling Helen, I love you, God Bless you and look after you.

CHAPTER 7

Andromada

Imeditated. Mary and Philip were there and took me to see KH. KH was sitting at the oval glass table. She wanted me to look at the table. I looked and a holographic image appeared in the middle, it was of the earth. KH was explaining to me the importance of The Birth of Light. She then stood up and took my hand, we were going to pay a visit somewhere. We flew out through the window. Surprise, I have wings. We approached another planet which was surrounded in pink.

On landing, amazed to find a small stream with a waterfall. We sat on the ground by the stream and I looked around. This indeed was a strange place. A house on stilts was not far from us. None of the surrounding ground had been harmed by this structure. I couldn't figure out how to get into the house as there were no steps up or even a door.

KH started to draw a sign in the sand. This sign is below (Figure Five in centre pages). She mentioned that this was important and one day I would understand the meaning of this sign.

Then joy a figure approached, it was My Lord. I smiled. This time I was allowed to hug My Lord. Oh! how I love Him.

We had two weeks holiday coming up and hadn't planned to go away anywhere. We had an invite to go and see John in Dorset, also an invite to Bedford to see a member of BEAMS, British Earth and Air Mysteries Society.

Ken ran the Bedford Branch of BEAMS and had written an article in the same magazine as my article. Ken had invited me down to give a talk to his society in October of this year and wished to meet me beforehand.

However, that fortnight's holiday was very important, as I was about to find out.

May and Phil came to the house and I taught them how to heal the energy. Both were able to dowse with the rods. However, due to

Phil's illness he was not able to crystal dowse on the map as his hand shook so much. But this did not deter him and he completed a healing. But I did notice that some parts of Wales were now reverting back to being negative.

There is no point in healing the energy on the land, if the people remain negative. Remember, every thought, word and deed creates energy in the cycle of the universe. Therefore, I could now see the point Merlin was making about teaching the people. In other words, he is right, this knowledge is for everybody.

One of May's original sins was in Castle Coch (See Picture Six in centre pages). May told me that she was drawn to the castle and had visited many times. By now, I had written some instruction sheets, Oh about five pages to help people with eradication of original sin, which also explained about the energy and how to use it through the colours. I gave her the instruction sheets.

I felt that May picked up more of the emotion on the healing. I knew that in the future she would be able to read people herself.

May was worried about Phil's condition. I reassured her that he would have his transplant this year, middle to the end of October. God moves in mysterious circles. Phil would be healed and I could see that he himself would become a healer. It was like he had to go through this experience to understand what others would go through. I believe that in the future, his destiny lay with teaching and healing the young people of the next generation.

I had already experienced myself the wisdom of those words. The reasons why I had to go through the persecution of the lower levels when first becoming a medium.

One girl suffered badly. My faith never let me down, it was because of my faith in God, in those days, that I recovered so quickly. This girl had no faith.

In effect, I was helping her by my own experiences. Showing her a way, through God, to help herself. This girl had already seen past life original sins and not knowing what was happening to her became suicidal.

I am glad to say that she has since recovered and through finding God was able to cope and is now learning the levels.

That night I decided to heal Wales again, as obviously, parts had reverted back to negative in such a short space of time. One spot stood out. It was a few miles outside Brecon Town. The following day it was back negative again. So, on healing this spot again, I decided, if it reverted back I would make a visit to the place.

I meditated.

Merlin was there with two angels. They escorted me to see KH. This time, more people were sitting at the table. I was allowed to, not only see them, but be introduced. My Lord stood up. I can never get used to the fact that I see My Lord so often in meditation. I love Him.

I was introduced to Mendassa. He explained, he was a bit like Merlin but in charge of other planets. In fact, five planets!!

Other planets? Did I hear correct?

Mendassa was dressed in turquoise and he did look like everybody's impression of Merlin. A long flowing gown with a pointy hat. He had a long beard which was grey. Again, he was very tall like Merlin.

KH asked me to sit down and she explained. I was now to be instructed by a Cosmic Thunder Being, called Andromada. Andromada would teach me all about the other worlds and also knowledge to help Mother Earth.

Andromada had apparently asked to be with me and it was agreed.

A door opened and a vision of loveliness walked in escorted by two angels.

Her waist long hair is golden but as she walks in, I could see that soft tones of pink showed through. Her eyes are pale pink but it is her dress that was stunning. It sparkled like diamonds in shades of rose pink, gold and silver. The whole effect, from a distance, was like a salmon colour. Again, she is tall and oh so beautiful.

Andromada was introduced to me as my new guide. We looked at each other, I was lost for words. KH said there was one more thing. The work I was about to do was important but I would be attacked by the negative/dark forces. Apparently, once I started on this new work they would be aware and will attack. Oh! great, that's all I need.

My Lord stood up and took his Crown of Thorns from his head. My Lord came over to me and placed the Crown of Thorns on my head and explained that when I was being attacked the Crown would let me know. He went on. Not everybody is aware that they are being attacked. The dark/negative forces use people around you to stop the work progressing. These people will not be aware it is happening to them. This Crown will let you know when you are being attacked.

'Do not judge, as you will be aware that other forces are using them, it is not their fault.' My Lord went on. 'It takes a strong person to resist these forces, so it is important that you do not judge.'

I was overwhelmed. Again, I thought was this true. I was about to find out.

I checked the map again. It was negative.

I sat down to watch television with Chris trying to take my mind off the map. All of a sudden, every thought in my head was negative. Hang on, that's not me. I felt the sides of my head ache, The Crown - it was letting me know. I concentrated and felt the negative messages. I was being psychically attached.

I had kept a lot to myself because Chris is skeptic. On this occasion, I needed him. I told Chris what was happening but instead of helping he was furious. He told me I had to close down and stop the work I was doing. I knew the work was important but Chris' attitude was strange.

I remembered what My Lord had said about the negative/dark forces using people around me and wondered if they were using Chris. That night I felt alone, truly alone. As always I return to prayer. The aching ceased and I knew I was free.

I lay awake. Perhaps Chris was right, I should close down for a while.

I felt it, beautiful, a feeling of love. Andromada is on such a high vibration that all you feel when she is near is pure love.

Andromada has a lot to tell me.

There are hundreds of planets all in different stages of evolution. Earth is the seventh planet and the planet of emotions. Some planets are on a higher vibration and therefore a different dimension to earth. Others are on the same dimension, but in different stages of evolution. If one sees physical craft i.e. unusual sightings in the sky, UFOs, the beings are on the same dimensional level but a different physical level. In simple terms, as Merlin says, the ABC:-

Earth is on the same dimensional level as physical UFOs but the UFOs have obviously more technical knowledge.

The lights that phase in and out are on a different dimensional level, a higher vibration.

Andromada explained that the higher vibration the level, the higher the spiritual level. Andromada is a Thunder Being and was very spiritual. Therefore, she was on a high vibration. Andromada also explained that the reason I could see her was the fact that in meditation I had achieved, through the teaching, a high vibration.

Only those physical beings on this earth with spiritual help and guidance can reach the higher levels of vibration and could see the higher beings. Also, those working on the higher levels were able to feel and see more.

Apparently, when you become a crown shakra the work involved is on a high spiritual level. Andromada also told me that we do not die, we are all light beings. When our physical body dies we return to spirit. Our spirit then is judged, but not by God. As spirit we return to our higher souls and judge ourselves. Of course, we are all guided and helped in this process.

It is then up to our spirit if we wish to return or go on. Andromada explained that if we had achieved eradication of our sins on this planet we are allowed to go up a level and experience a higher level planet. So, in effect, there are no aliens. They are all learning, just like us, all part of the One God.

I thought of Hilary and her experiences of abduction. Andromada explained that this planet was allowed to do this work as it was helping their species. In fact, these beings were used by another race, which in effect, harmed them.

It has been decided by the Council that they had gathered enough genetic material to solve their problems. if they abducted after this decision was made then the planet would accumulate bad karma. These beings apparently understood this. Remember, the Universal Law of Karma.

Andromada told me that the earth was in a very precarious position as it was very negative and could, in effect, create holocausts and destroy itself. The concern of this planet and its negative people has given rise to alien intervention and not all of it good.

So God in His infinite wisdom has sent his angels to teach, preach and heal. Not only were the people to be healed but also the land. These are the spiritual teachers and there are sixty four of them, they are Cosmic Light Beings and you are one of them. Andromada told me that I was a very old soul and had experienced living in most the planets. She explained that a lot of the older souls had returned to earth to help. The first step for me was memory. This, Andromada explained, is where she is going to help.

Each and every negative physical person was to have a positive spirit guide to help them obtain enlightenment. Mother Earth has a soul and she has been crying out for help. With our cosmic friends, Mother Earth had been drawing in the corn to attract, not only the counsel's attention, but also to wake people up and make them consciously aware.

Andromada also told me that there were very negative forces working on the spiritual level of this planet to stop the changes that would be happening. As soon as I commenced the next step, I would be involved in that spiritual battle. Whosoever won that battle, wins the physical earth.

In the Orion system there are many planets, some dark/negative and some light. Some of the planets have beings of both light and dark and are experiencing their own spiritual battle at the present time.

Both forces are at work on this planet at the moment. The Orion system had beings that were on the same dimensional level as earth but not on the same evolution. They are far more advanced technically than earth. Their craft or space ships are often seen.

Both negative and positive forces have been involved with the Americans, Russians and main world organisations. So be warned, as not all the physical spacecraft are here to help us, some are here to create chaos and misinformation.

Also, some of the Orion light beings are here as astral projections, acting as positive guides.

The Sirians are also here. Andromada knows some Sirians. They too, are on a very high vibration and appear as lights. The Sirians are in a different dimension and appear as lights in the sky which phase in and out. In meditation, I have seen the Sirians as golden people.

Andromada went on. In the Pleiades system there are again many planets with different beings, both positive and negative.

I couldn't believe my ears. I stopped Andromada as I had so many questions.

'Andromada, if I am a Cosmic Light Being then how come I had original sin?'

Andromada explained that I have been on this planet since the beginning, to learn. In learning, I had to experience every emotion, whether good or bad. To get to this stage I had to experience every situation in order that I could become a spiritual teacher in the necessary time of change in earth's history.

In effect, nothing was good and nothing was bad, but all a learning experience. With each difficult life situation, remember, it is a learning package from God. It is the way that you open this package is the way that you learn.

Remember also, The Universal Law of Karma, whatever you do in your life will come back on you, in one form or another.

Andromada explained that earth history was older that we could ever imagine. That all planets have the energy grid system and that is why a lot of the spaceships are built to accommodate that energy as fuel. That is why large energy centres are frequently visited by alien spacecraft.

The pyramids in Egypt are large energy centres. Andromada also told me that they were dimensional doorways. In fact, most energy centres were these doorways.

I couldn't believe all the information she gave me. It seems that now I was going on a very strange pathway indeed. However, I still kept my faith. Every morning and every night I said my prayers. Use me, My Father, as a vessel of Your peace.

The following morning, the start of our holidays. Great, fantastic.

Chris and I decided, first of all a rest as we both felt we needed it.

By the afternoon, I was restless. I felt a tingling and then pure love.

'Hi, Andromada.' I said to an empty room. 'I love you.'

Andromada asked me to get the atlas out of the world. I found the book and enquired what next. 'Open the book, Jane, to the Americas.' I did as I was instructed. 'Now I would like you to bring in the crystal colour orange.' I did as I was instructed, I knew Andromada was helping me with the crystal colour.

'Now do your healing on one State, one State only this afternoon.'

I was panicking inside. 'A whole State!! Andromada?' She was gone. The negativity of Wales alone made me so tired, I had slept for quite a few hours afterwards. Not only that, all that negativity - I remembered York.

However, if this is what My Father wishes me to do, who am I to argue with Him. The cards helped, the seven of fire came out. This card is represented by courage. The meaning of the car is as follows:-

Conditions intensify. Take further risks with greater awareness. The reality of the past no longer works for you. If you trust in your own internal convictions, you will develop strengths and a sense of self-confidence which will work for you. If you have the courage of your convictions, all that traps you will fall away.

Also the Birth of Light card came out as well as the Enlightenment card. I was on the right path.

I healed a State. I felt the energy rush. I lay down on the sofa. Father please give me the strength to take the negativity. I felt Him. I felt My Lord. I closed my eyes and I saw Him. He placed His cape over me. Next, I saw Merlin and he too took off his cape and placed it over me. I felt safe and fell asleep.

Over the next week, I was to heal, as Andromada calls it, The Americas. In the cards I was rewarded the Resurrection card came out.

This card means:-

Resurrection into a new way of thinking. You are entering into a new direction in life, which will be replaced by a deep understanding and enlightenment. The change that has occurred or will occur you have earned. You deserve the rewards that you receive.

I have noticed when this card comes out I seem to acquire a new skill. This occasion was no different.

Merlin told me that I could now use psychometry. Psychometry is where a clairvoyant can pick up information about people by merely holding an item of their personal possession. It works.

In addition, I was to have a new guide to help me. Doctor Chan is a Mandarin, a great healer with herbs and also a very good clairvoyant.

Doctor Chan is unusual to say the least. He always bows when I ask for his help. He is dressed in a Chinese outfit of yellow, orange and gold and has a small yellow hat on his head. He is the most perfect gentleman. He is never wrong.

On one occasion, I met Hilary in the Health Club and we went in the sauna. A young girl was sitting on the top bench. I could see she was distressed and asked for her ring. I asked Doctor Chan to help, which he did. He told me that she had attended college for a beauticians course, which was not successful as she didn't listen. Doctor Chan tells me the truth, he doesn't hold his punches.

This girl was too busy having a good time and talking through the lessons. However, he did see an opportunity for her in a night school course which would lead to her having her own business. If only I had the courage and confidence to tell her all of that. I started with the night school course for Aromatherapy.

'Strange,' she said. 'I took a beauticians course in college.'

Well what can I say, except he's good.

Through the rest of the week I worked through all the countries of the world. Until, one day on waking up after one session, I had a vision.

I saw a colour, a kind of lime mist. In this mist, I saw a throne, My Father. My Father was sitting on this throne. For one brief second I had seen My Father.

I was excited and I felt honoured. 'Andromada, Merlin,' I called. Instantly they were there. 'Did I really see what I think I saw?'

Merlin confirmed that it was so. Andromada told me that the colour, God's colour, was the next step. I was to bring in that colour as a form of crystal. This was difficult but I managed it. When I brought in the colour to fill the pyramid over and under me, it changed. The middle of the pyramid was brilliant white. The sides of the pyramid had encrusted diamond shaped gems all over it. These gems were emerald and yellow. His special colour was a dimensional crystal colour.

This colour I was to use on the central pages of the atlas. A picture spread over two pages, the whole world. Don't get me wrong I was scared. It took a lot of courage and my faith in God to complete that healing. But I was rewarded, the earth's energy was now positive. My healing along with others doing this work had turned the earth positive. This was confirmed to me by another who was healing at the same time.

I felt it. It was like time had stopped for me. I felt paralysed and heavy and then all of a sudden, woosh, one of the biggest energy surges I had ever felt. I closed my eyes and saw darkness. In the darkness I saw light, lifting up slowly at first, then my whole vision was taken up with light. It made me quite dizzy and I opened my eyes. Woosh, another energy surge.

I needed strength to take this. I was very frightened. As I thought it - they were there, all of them. Mary was first, I felt her enter me, then Philip. As each one came I felt them enter me until I knew nothing could touch me.

God's colour is very strong and I use is sparingly. The next morning, I was fine. The negativity had not effected me. I had received so much strength from my friends, Oh how I love them all.

There is only one person I have taught this colour to. She is very special, her name is Ali.

I met Ali in the Health Club, she worked there as a physiotherapist. One day she saw me do the cards for Hilary and asked if I would read her cards.

In her cards, I could see her soul was in torment and looking for direction. I also saw that she was on the beauty path. The beauty path is one in tune with nature, loving all God's creations. She told me she had booked a holiday to go alone to America. This, she explained, was to find herself. I knew different. America was where her original sins were, in fact, the last ones. I gave her the instruction sheets to explain more and knew, one day, she would go to America and never return home.

I healed her and taught her how to bring in God's energy through the colours. She thanked me in her usual way, a hug and a kiss. She is so beautiful, inside and out.

Ali went to America and told me afterwards she felt at home spiritually. Of course she would, it was her natural home. I felt that around her she had her own guides, Indian Guides. On returning from her holiday, Ali asked if she could come up the house to learn more.

I taught her how to heal the land with a map and crystal and I knew that she would, one day, learn all I had learned as she was to help open a Light Centre in America. A Light Centre is where, in the future, all types of healing will take place.

In fact, Ali invited me to talk to more people and to teach. After the talk I told her I had something special to show her. God's light, His dimensional crystal colour. I told her nothing and just asked if she could pick it up. As I pushed the light in she closed her eyes.

Ali feels a lot and I knew she would be able to pick it up. I wasn't disappointed. She told me it had a sparkly taste just like a sherbet dab. The colour she told me is a sort of yellow and green and as it came in it looked like prisms.

I had already healed the States of America but what better way for Ali to help. I told Ali that a spiritual battle was going on and would she like to help by making sure those States remained positive.

I also explained the importance of not taking in too much negativity at any one time, so perhaps, she would like to try and heal one State by using God's special colour. If she had problems to contact me, otherwise, to carry on with the work until all of America had been done. I warned her not to attempt any more that one State per day.

I was worried about her but I knew I would see her the following week.

We had many trips over that holiday, one to Bath Abbey another to West Wales to visit castles. Wherever I went, I healed the energy and released trapped spirits.

One trip was to The Cerne Abbas Giant in Dorset (See figure Two, centre pages). This huge chalk figure dominates a Dorset hillside. He represents an early Celtic God, some say he represents Hercules. It is believed to be over 2000 years old and is 180 feet tall. At the top of a steep hill, it would be, is the centre of the energy. It is above the giants head, slightly to the right. Needless to say we made the climb but I must admit, I must be getting fitter as it wasn't too bad.

What a disappointment, the giant is completely fenced off. Merlin told me it was all right, we could still open up the energy centre as we were not far from the right spot.

This giant is connected with local legends of fertility and up until 1635, a maypole was set up above the giant. Courting couples still make night time pilgrimages up the hillside to ensure that their marriages will be fruitful.

I have noticed that many of the older sites have been fenced off. It is such a shame. A lot of the churches I have been sent to for healing are closed and locked. This is our heritage and should be open to the people, especially God's house.

CHAPTER 8

The Spiritual Battle

I meditated. This time someone different came to fetch me. It was Mary, but not my Mary. I felt so much at peace, a feeling of reverence. This was Mary Magdalene. Mary Magdalene has none of the emotional traits that my Mary had. I felt that a truly religious person was standing before me.

Mary Magdalene is dressed in a nuns outfit. She is truly serene. Mary takes me to the white cathedral. I feel that this is a solemn and holy occasion.

At the top, by the altar, all my friends are waiting and some I didn't know. Mary stopped. On the floor lay the sign (figure two), the one I had seen in meditation. A circle with the eight points marked off.

Mary indicated that I should stand in the centre of this circle, which I did. Mary stood on one point and I saw each of my friends walk up and stand on the other points.

There was Andromada, Merlin and Mendassa but the others I did not, at this stage know. Each were represented by a colour. Andromada is rose pink, the sign of love. Merlin is purple/blue, intellect and healing. KH is pure white.

The others I was to meet at a later date. I now have many guides and know that I can call on them for help. However, I first have to meet them in order that I can learn about them.

Even at this stage you have to know who you are talking to. I still kept a vigil for that old devil.

When the circle was complete, I just knew instinctually what was going to happen. KH was first, her energy in a white beam flowed up the line and entered me. As each colour of energy entered me, I felt so strong. The eight colours made one beam of white light. This beam I was to use on the world. A holographic image of the world was before me. I started at the bottom and felt the white beam come out of the palm shakra and go into the world.

When I reached the top the world looked beautiful, a sparkly white oval shape. When I brought my hands back down it took away the white light and with it the old negative energy. I felt the power. I had never in my life experienced anything so powerful. But I was worried. This process was taking away some of the worst negativity which had accumulated for centuries. I knew that this negative energy I would have to channel.

I came out of the meditation and went to bed.

I woke up around 2.00 AM in the morning. My crown felt on fire. I started to pray. Afterwards, in my mind, I kept saying 'I have faith in God, who strengthens me, I have faith in God, who strengthens me.' I fell asleep.

The following morning, I felt tired but the aching on my crown had ceased.

I carried on with this form of healing on the world the following week and each time felt the power in my hands. What struck me was that my dream all those years ago was now coming true. I was helping to heal the world through the power of my hands with a white light.

I tell everybody to pay attention to their dreams. I think everybody has the ability to become psychic. Our dreams are important. It is a way that spirit can communicate with us. Remembering is the hardest part.

One night, after doing my usual work on the world, I woke again at 2.00 AM in the morning. Only this time it was different. I have never been so scared, the last time was when the devil came to me.

I opened my eyes and I saw consciously about fifteen dimensional tunnels in the bedroom. Help! Here we go again! What is happening? On the ceiling are three small tunnels. I was fascinated with the three small tunnels, they were gold on the outside and white on the inside with a line of silver.

What on earth was happening. I was drawn to the one tunnel by the window and coming down was a man!! He was dressed in a white tunic. On the front of the tunic there were arrows pointing upwards. He was tall and I could see that he had dark hair which was slightly going grey at the sides. That was it! That was enough for me! I woke Chris up and urgently told him to get downstairs. I fled.

Surprising what fear can do for you. Chris and I battled, he was furious. This time, he said, I will close down. I backed off as I was badly scared and agreed. I just knew that I had seen and felt a spiritual battle in my bedroom between the dark and light forces. I quickly agreed.

Chris calmed down. He could see I was badly scared. He felt this was way out of his league and needed help. I was adamant, I was not going back to that bedroom. I telephoned a medium in Wiltshire who was doing similar work and left a message on her answering machine. Chris telephoned Dave.

Now remember, this is 2.00 o'clock in the morning. A very sleepy voice answered the telephone. Chris asked Dave if he could come down and try to hypnotise me in order for me to calm down.

Bless him, he never refuses to help anyone. Dave arrived and spoke to Chris. I was in the front room watching another dimensional doorway. They are fascinating. I think the two men thought I was round the bend.

Dave tried to hypnotise me but it was unsuccessful. However, it did calm me down and I was able to see the channelling take place. It was like a white mist going up a ringed tunnel. In this mist were all kinds of things. I was very grateful for Dave to come down at that time in the morning, he is truly a good friend.

I turned to my faith, as usual, and asked My Father to help me sleep, it worked.

The following evening the medium telephoned. Thank goodness, I am not going mad -she had experienced the same thing. The spiritual battle which was going on was slowly being won by the light force but unfortunately, the dark/negative forces were throwing everything at the psychics who were helping. She told me that Merlin could help close down the negative dimensional doorways, all I had to do was ask him.

In addition, to help with the vibration that kept those doors closed to use two crystals, obsidian and black turmerlin. Obsidian clears away subconscious obstacles allowing clarity of thought and an understanding of silence. It is a powerful healer and turns any negativity into light. Turmerlin has very similar properties.

So, Merlin and I went through the house. Unbeknown to me, there was a very large cosmic doorway in the small front bedroom which Merlin put a double lock on, as this was negative. Merlin went on to explain that the three small doorways in the ceiling were Sirian and not to worry as they were looking after me. Merlin stated, I was lucky this race were very spiritual and like Andromada were pure love.

Five in the bedroom were Orion. However, Merlin left one door open from the Orion as they were positive. I understand now what it is like living on an energy centre. They must be really laughing at us looking for spaceships/UFOs when all they have to do is go through a dimensional doorway into this world. Merlin also explained there was a Pegasus doorway as well. Well, I'd never encountered any Pegasus beings. Merlin said I would in the future.

The next step, Merlin said, was a visit to a crystal shop. He wanted to come with me and help choose the crystals.

So the very next day I went shopping for crystals. The obsidian and tumerlin I found quite easily. Merlin then directed me to the rock crystal. I placed the obsidian in my palm and tried to read it like someone's personal possession. Wow! I could really feel it. The rock crystal was amazing, I felt my crown opening. Merlin explained that this would help me focus the energy.

Since finding out I can actually feel the energy in different crystals I've been like a kid testing everything I touch. Do you know that trees have the most beautiful feeling. I had forgotten that every living thing contains this energy and that is what I was picking up. It was like being reborn, having another sense to use.

I tested everything I could get me hands on. Each living thing has an energy code, a different vibration , you could even say a musical note. Some stones' vibration had increased and become different due to it's environment.

Chris reminded me of my promise to close down. I was sad but I had to keep my promise.

'Think of it as a holiday,' said Chris.

So, I asked Merlin to show me a way to close down, it worked. Oh! misery. I had peace all right but without picking up on the energy I couldn't read the cards. I felt so tired all the time. After a few days I couldn't take it any more. Chris could see the change and agreed.

'OK, have it your way, open up again if you wish,' he said.

If I wished, I was ecstatic. I missed my friends. So Merlin helped me open up again. I was like a kid.

I spent the next couple of weeks experimenting trying all types of crystals, trees, stones etc. It was a new experience and quite exciting.

When I next saw Ali, I couldn't believe it, she was in a bad way. Our Father is wise, you have to experience a situation before you can help others. Ali had experienced the spiritual battle and I was able to show her a way through it. Ali picked up straight away on the crystals. I gave her the rock crystal that Merlin had chose, she needed something to help her focus.

I also directed her to the obsidian and tumerlin.

Ali asked if she could come to the house again to learn more. I was delighted.

I also telephoned the medium in Wiltshire to thank her for her help. One of her guides is Sitting Bull, a reincarnation of Merlin. No wonder she knows so much about me. Out of the blue she asked I would like to spend a weekend with her. I was delighted. Here was my chance to learn more.

Merlin took me shopping, a present for staying the weekend. This medium had told me more about the Sirians. She told me that if a Sirian was around me I was lucky. The Sirians used crystal colours, their favourite being rose pink, gold and silver. On shopping, I saw a slate Celtic Cross with these colours.

'No,' said Merlin. 'The colour you need is blue.' So I chose a blue Celtic Cross with gold.

I was nervous about going to a place, not knowing anyone and not knowing what to expect. So, I said my prayers. Oh! I tingled all over again. I knew who this was. A voice told me to pick out a book from the ones on the sideboard. I obeyed. I felt for the book and knew it as soon as I touched it.

'This book you must take with you, it is for the medium. Now, Jane, I want you to choose another book.' I obeyed again.

'Whose book is this?' I asked My Father. Immediately, a picture came into my mind. It was for a tall, young man. Light brown hair and it looked like a beard, or perhaps he hadn't shaved.

I have to tell you I feel very honoured when that happens. These people must be very special.

So armed with the books and The Celtic Cross I went to Wiltshire. I had with me a sleeping bag and a fresh change of clothes. I was lucky, a friend offered to drive me there and Chris would pick me up.

We had no trouble in finding the right place. The medium had told me, that if it was meant to be I wouldn't have any trouble. Apparently, others had tried to visit but were not successful in finding the place.

I liked her straight away. Merlin had told her we each had something to give to the other. I don't know what I gave her as she was definitely further along the path than me. We talked most of the afternoon. She was delighted with the cross and told me it was her colour. The peace in her house was lovely. After being so long in this battle, it was respite, a time for calming down.

A young man called in the evening along with a friend. You guessed it. This was the young man I was shown. I told him the story of the book and gave it to him. He was special. In the evening the energy built up and the medium told us a Pegasus Being was in the room. I felt it but I could not see. Apparently, Pegasus are silver with green eyes.

The following morning the medium explained that I needed grounding. Apparently, my spirit was off astral travelling with all my cosmic friends whilst my physical body slept. She asked if lately my ears were popping. She was correct, I had noticed myself in the last few months. She said that the reason why they were popping - galactic travelling!!

I hadn't heard from Merlin for a week. The medium said that wasn't the case, he had spoken to me early Saturday morning. Ah yes, I remember now. I had a strange dream. I was in a chair and these men were trying to put electrons on my head. In front of me was a monitor. They were recording what I was doing. I remember telling Merlin about it. I had wrenched off the electrons and ran under what looked like a table and then woke up.

Merlin was furious. 'I'm not having that,' he said and was gone. Before I left for Wiltshire he showed me a key. The key opened the last Orion dimensional doorway.

'A dream?' the medium said, as if to question the fact it was a dream.

The medium confirmed that Mary Magdalene was with me, along with Merlin and Andromada. Apparently, she saw Andromada's dress. Before leaving, she told me that more Thunder Beings would be with me in the near future.

I haven't mentioned your name, but bless you. You gave me peace when I needed it most. I now know, I only have to pick up the telephone and you will help. I will remember you and hope to visit you again in the future. God bless you and keep you. I thank My Father that there are understanding people like you around, every ready with open arms.

I returned home, happy and content, ready for the next battle.

I had to prepare for Bedford. I was to give a conference in Bedford for about sixty to seventy people. Both Chris and Dave were coming. Chris was going to record the speeches made by Dave and myself.

CHAPTER NINE

The
Bedford Conference

We were leaving early in the morning in order to have time to talk with Ken before the conference started.

The night before, I prepared. I was gathering my things that I would need. I hoped to ask for a volunteer to give a small demonstration. This volunteer I was going to teach to dowse and pick up on the energy in front of the others. I would be looking for someone who had never dowsed before. In addition, I was going to take the tape that Chris had made which gave more information.

The back room vibrated and I heard a voice. 'Choose two books, Jane, like before.' I obeyed and asked who the books were for. 'One is for Ken, the other is for Anne.' A picture of Anne came into my mind. The voice carried on. 'Anne will become a spiritual leader for her area. You will also need holy water.'

'Holy water!' I replied. It was too late to go to the only church I knew was open but even there the font was dry.

'You will be helped.' My Father replied. I can never get used to that, I love Him.

The vibration changed and Andromada was there. 'Fill a small bottle up with water, it has to be glass.' Andromada directed me to a small bottle which came with a cross. This cross had been Chris' family cross, they were Catholics.

I did as I was instructed and filled the bottle up with water. Hold the bottle, Andromada told me and close your eyes. I closed my eyes and saw her, she is beautiful, but she stepped aside and then I saw My Lord. My Lord came over to where I was sitting and I felt him enter me. What a feeling, what joy.

I felt the soft power flow through, through my arms into the bottle through my palm shakras. Just as suddenly as they were there, they were gone. I was left holding a bottle and a very special memory.

Whenever I am down or depressed I hold that bottle and feel the energy of My Lord, it always works. I can never feel down as long as I know He is there.

I said my prayers that night and asked for a volunteer to help with the demonstration. I know inside my prayers will be answered as I was doing My Father's work.

Dave was the navigator and we got lost a couple of times. However, we arrived safely and met Ken. I took to Ken straight away, I knew I would.

Ken took us to a flat in the centre where the talks were to be held and introduced us to Emily. What a lady. What a beautiful person. She was small and dainty and full of spirituality. I gave her a reading and then she proceeded to give me a reading as she too was psychic. We were not alone, I felt Him, He was there. I saw Him and then he entered me.

Forgive me Emily, I never told you. Who would have believed me. But she did say to me, 'I see the Son in you.' He was directing me now. I got out the small bottle of holy water and on opening it asked her to taste it. I saw a look in her eyes, a look of recognition.

'I have tasted this before,' she said. 'The Tears of Christ.' She went away and got out a story she had written many years ago.

I will give you a brief outline of that true story.

One day a scrap merchant found a picture of Christ holding a small coloured child. He had found the picture up in the attic of his house when he had a clear out. The picture, he decided, was going to be thrown away and took it out into the garage. In the garage the picture mysteriously caught fire and the fire spread to his arm. Beating out the flames, he decided to bring the picture back into the house.

As the picture by now was charred he left it on the kitchen floor and he and his wife went to bed. He had decided to leave the picture where it was until morning.

In the morning the picture was fully restored to it's original condition. The scrap merchant was amazed. He was not that religious and wondered why he had been chosen. Later in the day the picture cried tears. It was a miracle. That day he told everybody about the picture, including Emily.

The picture continued to cry tears. This water was gathered up and put into bottles. Whosoever called at the house to see the picture, which they did, took away the holy water. Emily is an accomplished artist and asked if she could paint the picture in oils. That picture was given to a very holy person who kept it on her sideboard.

Emily had recognised my holy water as that from the picture.

I also gave Ken a reading and saw that his partner in life had a different view on religion. Also, the time spent in his research work was resented. However, in the future their paths would cross and they would become like one.

I directed him to writing, especially for his own magazine. Ken was very much on the spiritual path and his enquiring mind was seeking knowledge. Ken asked if I would show him how to heal the land. It was decided that we do this in the hall that was to be used for the conference. Good. I wanted to heal the energy around us.

Ken was able to pick up the energy and dowse. He healed an area near where he lived. I wanted peace to do my prayer work and sat quietly out of the way. Chris and Dave were setting up the video cameras. Dave had also brought his camera.

People started to arrive and I spoke to one or two before Dave started his speech. I couldn't see Anne. I had given Ken his book and explained how important it was. The book was published in 1917 and there were six pages of the original author's notes attached. It was indeed a special book.

I went outside to get some fresh air. People were still arriving. I was drawn to a group that had just arrived, one of the women particularly. Anne had not arrived but Ken told me that this woman I was drawn to, was her partner. They owned a book shop which also sold crystals. Anne was into spiritual healing. I had the right person to give the other book to. He never lets me down. I know, one day, I will return to Bedford to meet Anne.

Dave's speech was on his UFO investigations in the Cardiff and surrounding areas. He also included his work in hypnotherapy. It was very interesting and very well received.

It was my turn. I was very nervous but I knew I was not alone. I put on the video first of all and then taught the audience how to bring in God's energy in the three colours, pink, blue and white.

'Who tingles?' I asked. Most people put up their hands and I asked for a volunteer.

Well, afterwards Chris said he would like to wrap this volunteer up and put him in the boot of the car for each conference I attend. He was marvellous. His name was Philip, bless you Philip for volunteering. He had never dowsed in his life and was not only able to pick up the energy but dowse with the rods and crystals.

I noticed when I pushed the blue light through him there was a muddy spot over the right hand side of his head. I knew this had to be stress. Also, a black line showed on both knees and this was arthritis. Philip confirmed the diagnosis. By his own dowsing was able to confirm also that he had two original sins.

He completed a healing on an Ordnance Survey map of the Bedford area. The crystal went round in circles proving that he had completed his task. His hand also went warm on the healing. I then answered many questions from the audience and finally gave Anne's partner her book explaining how special it was.

Many people stayed around to talk and ask questions. I gave many healings and helped as many as I could. In fact, I run out of the instruction sheets which I had taken. Ken promised to photocopy more for those people who asked.

One young man I could see would become a very famous artist. He would paint what he sees. I was told, at the time, here is another William Blake. He was slightly off his path but still successful. I emphasised to him to paint what he sees.

Another young man approached. In him I saw me. In the future he would be on a stage giving talks.

Ken was curious, he didn't know I could see what was wrong with people and asked if I would check him out. Of course. I started at the top. He had stress and I could see tubes that were slowly clearing. This was due to a change in diet and a voice told me - he's gone vegetarian. Of course, this was helping a condition in his chest. Ken confirmed this. He also had a knee problem like Philip but this was getting worse. Physical exercise like swimming would help. Ken told me that he was constantly riding a bike to help the condition in his knees.

I enjoyed giving the talk and demonstration but was glad to be going home. I was tired. Always when I work psychically I get tired very easily.

Since visiting Bedford, I understand that Ken and Philip have teamed up and written a book. Good luck to you both. Send me a copy of your book when it is published and I'll sent you a copy of mine.

I meditated.

Mary and Philip were there with Merlin.

They escorted me to the white cathedral. Small children dressed in white were throwing flower petals at our feet. This must be a celebration.

We entered to a fanfare. KH was at the alter with all my friends. I had now met many more of them.

My mother was there looking radiant along with my aunt. I smiled, again, I felt this was not only a celebration but also a holy occasion.

I walked to the altar and noticed for the first time, I was a man!! I was dressed all in white, with a white cape which had a sparkly diamond lining. I looked at myself amazed, who was I?

KH explained, that I was disguised this physical lifetime as a woman. This was just like my book, The Guardian, the dream I had all those years ago when I was a teenager.

The work I was doing was very important and it had been decided, that to avoid detection by the dark/negative forces, I would come back, as I had requested, as a woman.

I knelt at the altar and KH held a Sword of Light which she proceeded to bring down through me. I felt it.

The story gets stranger. KH handed me the sword and asked me to do the same. KH knelt before me. I drew the sword and brought it down through her. I also felt that. I went to hand the sword back but she stopped me.

'This is the Sword of Light, it is yours. When you go to America strike it on the ground as you enter. The whole of the Americas will shudder and know you have arrived. Use the sword wisely, my child.'

I woke up. I felt beside me for the sword, I could feel it's vibration. I knew it was there.

I have accepted myself. We are all part of God and Christ is within all of us. We are all children of God.

Knowing that is easy. Accepting it is harder.

I now know that I have gone up another level and with it a new gift.

After the meditation, Andromada was there. Andromada had come to reach me my new gift.

'Tomorrow morning pick two roses from the garden. These roses are special, they must be deep rose pink.' She said and was gone.

The following morning I did as I was asked. I felt the vibration of love, Andromada was there. Pull the petals out and wash them. I did as I was told. 'Place them in a sealed glass container with water and a little oil. Then go into the back room.'

I lit a candle for Andromada and closed the door. I felt something very special was going to happen.

'Close your eyes, Jane. Is it all right if I enter you?' she asked. Of course it was, Andromada is pure love. I cannot describe how I felt but I will say it was a beautiful moment. As our minds entwined I knew exactly what to do. I focused the energy of Andromada, her very special energy vibration into the bottle through the palm shakras. I felt the bottle warm up.

All of a sudden it was over and I put the bottle down. 'Leave it a week.' Andromada said. Andromada went on to tell me that this would help people with depression as it was the essence of love.

Well, I was like a kid again waiting for something to brew. I couldn't wait to try it out. I looked at the bottle in the evenings, but I knew, I couldn't open it for a week.

That week passed slowly. The big day came and I opened up the bottle. I felt Andromada, but she wasn't there. I understand now. Everything has energy and vibration. Substances can be changed through focusing energy into it.

I squeezed the petals, I thought I was on a high. It really is very powerful. Andromada later explained that this was to go into the aura of a person. If you put a small amount on your hand and rub your hands together. Then place your hands around your body working about six inches away from your body you will feel it.

Andromada explained, that a person would have to be taught how to pick up on the energy in order to use any kind of aura preparation.

Merlin was quite excited. This, apparently, was a subject he loved. He directed me to a book 'The science of Crystals,' which I must admit I am only half way through. It is fairly easy to read but I have been busy. It is interesting and I note that quantum physics comes into it. I feel I am going to be quite learned by the time Merlin's finished.

Another book Merlin directed me to was 'The Power of Gemstones.' It seems that certain gemstones can be used for certain ailments. Obviously, by focusing the energy into water containing certain gemstones their vibration would be left in the water, thus, having healing abilities for specific ailments. The possibilities seemed endless.

Doctor Chan directed me to a book on practical modern herbal remedies. Of course, directing the focused energy into herbs. How about crystals and herbs. Well, the list is endless.

I have thoroughly enjoyed researching what herb and crystal can benefit different ailments.

I will give you a couple of examples:-

Oil of bluebell, water and sunflower oil - this has been used on many people. In aromatherapy it takes away all negativity and helps open up the shakras. I have also been told by Merlin it helps high blood pressure.

Rock crystal, lavender, water and sunflower oil - this helps kidney problems, promotes sleep - a general healer of wounds.

Both of the above examples have been used by people who have benefited. I have to emphasise that these were made with focused energy.

Merlin and Doctor Chan have been helping and guiding me in making these up. It seems they know when a person with an ailment will be directed to me, as they are prepared beforehand.

I made up the one for kidney problems for Phil.

May and Phil invited us to dinner. Oh May, you really spoiled us. The meal was beautiful. I only wish I had a bigger stomach so I could have eaten more. May you are a good cook and the meal was very much appreciated.

Phil and May were drawn to the spiritual path when Phil developed kidney problems.

May had already had some experiences herself. She had no fear of seeing. Well, I've got a surprise for you. You will see more in the future. You will be helped and guided by earth spirits to start with until you reach a higher level. Once this level is reached, you must realise that then you will have cosmic guides as well. Don't worry, I will always be there for you. You know you will only have to pick up the telephone and I will come running.

I opened up Phil and May's house and healed the energy. By placing a pyramid over the house, I filled it with blue crystal. This was to help Phil with his illness. Remember, blue for healing. I taught May how to do this and she tells me it makes a difference. In fact, when they took a holiday in Devon they couldn't sleep and felt restless.

May placed a pyramid over the caravan in which they were staying and felt a lot better afterwards.

May also told me that she had paid a visit to Castle Coch (See Picture Six, centre pages) to eradicate one of her original sins. She had difficulty walking up to the castle and felt she was going to have an asthma attack. Something she had not suffered with for years. However, once she was inside, she knew exactly where to go. May asked forgiveness of her sin. May told me that one she felt she had been forgiven for her sin all her ailments immediately disappeared.

One day I had a telephone message from May. 'Jane, what is it like to always be right.' Apparently, Phil had been called into hospital for his kidney transplant. He went in 17th October, remember, middle to end of October as I had predicted. Well, I can't take credit for that one as my guides were helping me.

Bless you both. I know that you are very special. Both of your lives are going to change.

Every life leaning experience can be a blessing in disguise. It is the way you learn, sometimes through life's tragedies that you realise it was all part of His plan.

Chapter Ten

The Celtic Cross

Merlin told me I was to receive a reward for all the work I have done. But first, a visit was necessary to two places. One was Brecon and the other Neath.

Brecon is a National Park with approximately 519 square miles of hills, sheer mountainsides, moorlands, lakes, streams and caves. It is a very beautiful place.

Brecon town is an old market town with narrow streets. It contains a medieval castle and a 13th century fortified cathedral. Also, there is a Mountain Centre approximately three miles from Brecon Town.

As you know, I have had problems with this area and was a bit apprehensive to say the least. Chris said he would take me and we arrived at the Mountain Centre early in the afternoon. I healed the energy and leys at the centre. I felt it. The Mountain Centre overlooked many mountains and I could feel them all opening up. No problems yet.

There was a craft fair at the Mountain Centre and we had a look around. One woman was making pictures from melted, coloured wax. They were truly stunning. Most of the pictures were of dolphins and sea scenes. I asked her if she had considered making a picture of the Celtic Cross. Then I said a very strange thing. 'Will you, one day, make a picture of a Celtic Cross for the cover of my book?' Well you could have knocked me down with a feather. I had started the book but had only just written the first chapter. I wonder why I asked that.

On leaving the Mountain Centre, I felt strange. On approaching Brecon town I had a strange dream, a conscious vision. I saw a monk, a young monk, breaking his vows of chastity with a beautiful young girl. Well, there's a fine mess. I felt that this scene was being relayed to me for a reason. I just knew that one of those players was me in a past life. So this is how I deviated!!

We didn't stay long in Brecon town but long enough for me to heal both the church and Christ College. I knew I was in the right place at Christ College and proceeded with the healing.

On returning home, I asked Merlin if this was one of my original sins. He told me that in that lifetime I was not the monk but the innocent young girl. In fact, in forgiving the monk I had set him free as guilt had kept him on the earth plane. Apparently, it was young love.

Neath Abbey was slightly different. I felt the malevolence as we turned into the street containing the ruined abbey. The ruins had been restored earlier this century and were quite beautiful. But, unfortunately, it was a soured well. There was something truly wrong with this place.

On walking around the ruins, which I might add is in a very prominent position, I felt an unbearable dread. The views all around were impressive; to one side were views of the Swansea coastline; another hills and lowlands. It was truly magnificent. I commenced My Father's work. However, on this occasion, it took many healings. It was not until I actually healed the church that I felt release. All the time, I knew, I was being watched but I dare not close my eyes as I would see what was watching.

On coming away from the abbey, I was content, another job done. I was not alone Merlin was with me. A ride along Neath Valley was called for. We were going to a waterfall. One thing I always wanted to do was to go behind a waterfall. This was my reward. In Neath Valley is a waterfall and yes, you guessed it, you can actually walk behind the waterfall. What a feeling. Chris captured the moment on his video camera.

I went to Spiritualist Church that Saturday evening but I had no messages. Strange, the medium kept picking on me but the messages were for someone else. May and Phil were there and asked if we would like to join them for a drink with their friends Sheila and Alec. We were delighted to.

Sheila was very easy to pick up on and I could see that she was psychic herself. One day, she too, would be reading people herself. Alec. Well, what can I say about Alec except he is a darling. I could see he was hard working and very talented. His hands were of an artist and his talent wasted. He was working all hours in a job that didn't become him. What could I do to help.

I was told there would be an opportunity for him part-time in a fresh field, this would open the door to his creative talents. But, unfortunately, he would miss this opportunity as it was part-time work and he would not entertain it.

What could we do to help. In my mind I was shown a book full of drawings. Alec was certainly talented and could carve in wood. I told Alec what I saw and he exclaimed that he had recently bought a book on carvings of the Celtic Cross. I'll have a think about this one.

One lunch hour, I paid a visit to the shop which sold the slate Celtic Crosses and asked the owner if he would be interested in wood carvings. He said he would. Next step.

I asked May if she would get in touch with Alec and ask him if it was possible to carve me a Celtic Cross. Alec knowing my spiritual interest would not have any suspicion as to the reasons why I wanted a wooden Celtic Cross.

I thought no more of it for a while.

The following weekend, I was drawn to a paper and on reading it found an article about Nevern in West Wales.

'In the churchyard at Nevern, there is an ancient tree known as Yr Ywen Waedlyd (The Bleeding Yew). A red liquid flows from it's trunk. Popular folk tradition maintains that a man, possibly a monk, was hanged on this tree. Before dying, he swore that the tree would bleed forever as evidence of his innocence.'

Also, in the same paper was another article about Nevern.

'A few yards from the church, a path leads to a small cross known as Croes y Pererinion, The Pilgrim's Cross, carved in the rock. The path was used by saints and pilgrims on their journey to St. David's. In the churchyard stands one of the finest Celtic Crosses in Wales.'

I asked the cards and they told me I was on the right path. So again, I asked Chris quite casually.

'Darling, can we go to West Wales tomorrow?'

Well Chris, by now, was getting used to me wanting to go up and down the country.

'Yes,' he replied. Isn't he great.

This was a long journey and it took us about four and half hours to reach our destination. I took holy water with me and also a preparation I had made with the focused energy.

On arriving at the churchyard in Nevern, I felt power. This time it didn't feel wrong, just powerful. The only other way I can describe it, is a heavy purple feeling. Large trees dominated the churchyard. I got out the holy water and made a sign of the cross on each tree and proceeded with the healing. When I had finished, I stood at the entrance of the church. The churchyard now felt a lot lighter, by the entrance to the church was the Celtic Cross.

The total height is 13 feet, the cross being 24 1/2 inches in diameter. The actual date is unknown. It is magnificent. Chris taped the healing and the Celtic Cross.

I was not alone. I tingled all over and felt it was Mary Magdalene.

'Jane, pick up the small, brown stone at the foot of the Celtic Cross. You will need this soon. This is the cross that must be carved.'

I look at it. Good Heavens! This is quite complicated and would be very difficult to carve in wood. The intricate design alone would take months to carve. Mary continued.

'When Alec has completed this task he will be a changed man. You must go to the Pilgrim's Cross, you will have a guide.'

Mary was gone. The church, surprisingly, was open as the cleaner was going about her duty. We entered the church, it is really worth a visit. On a table by the entrance there were little booklets explaining the history of the church. We paid for two as now, I knew, Alec would need one of them. Inside was an illustration of the Celtic Cross in the churchyard.

At the back of the church is a pathway over a stream. We proceeded over this pathway and up a hill to the woodland which contained The Pilgrim's Cross. The cross is cut in relief in the living rock and below it is a kneeling recess with a small incised cross. On the way up the hill we met a lady walking her dog. She stopped to talk. This lady explained, she was going to the woodland and would take us there. On the way she told us that she had searched for months for The Pilgrim's Cross and only came upon it by chance one morning.

Mary was right, we did have our guide. If it wasn't for this lady we would have also missed four footsteps which were carved in the rock further along the path. Inside these footsteps, three crosses were carved. I got out the holy water and also the preparation made with focused energy. I marked a cross, in holy water, at the foot of the Pilgrim's Cross and then poured some of the preparation on the kneeling stone.

Chris went further up the hill as I proceeded to get out my Prayer Book in order to read a prayer. What happened was another precious memory. I felt a very high vibration. This high vibration or energy was coming towards me. I closed my eyes and I saw the living Christ. I opened my eyes, He was there. Chris was walking down the pathway and was approaching. I turned to look at him and then back, He was gone.

We found the stone footprints without any trouble and again, I made the sign of the cross in each one with holy water. This indeed, was a very special place.

The lady had also told us about the end of the Pilgrim's Pathway. This ended a few miles down the road by an old ironwork bridge. We stopped at the bridge and as I walked over felt the energy released. It had poured with rain all the way across to West Wales and Chris had thought it was going to be a waste of time, but I was told that the rain would stop at Nevern, long enough to do the work. The rain had stopped during our visit but now it was getting dark and it had started to rain again. It was time to go home.

I told May about the Celtic Cross and she was confident that Alec would be able to carve such an intricate design. Alec has since contacted me looking for more material on the cross, as he feels it should be right. Also, he thought that this cross was a lot older than mentioned in the booklet, in fact, a good 2000 years older.

I looked in a reference book for the Celtic Cross in Nevern and sure enough it was there. Also, Chris recorded the cross on video when I healed Nevern. May and Phil invited us to their house along with Alec and Sheila to see if we could sort out the problem Alec was having with the carving of the Celtic Cross.

From a blown up picture of the Celtic Cross, Alec had drawn lines in order to calculate the dimensions. It suddenly dawned on me, I cannot believe it. The drawing represented the sign of the wheel that I have received in meditation (See Figure Five, centre pages). The Celtic Cross represents the eight points coming together in the middle for the ultimate 'One Birth of Light.' (See figure Six, centre pages) The central beam that heals the earth. Of course, the sign of infinity on the four points of the Celtic Cross representing the never ending circle. I cannot believe it. This race is so stupid to ignore all the signs that heaven give us. A mechanism which is ongoing to heal the negativity of our earth.

I had recently bought a Celtic Cross necklace and realised at the same time that this represented the key. (See figures Three and Four, centre pages) The three main healing colours; white for spirituality; blue for healing and pink for love. The key is turned in the eight point wheel.

I have also been told that this also represents the level of consciousness that the earth is presently at. All these signs had been drawn in the crop circles, all the levels of consciousness starting with the single crop circle. We have now reached level nine and the crop circles will now have the two examples as shown in figures Three and Five. Why? One, because this book has shown the mechanism on how to use the wheel/Celtic cross and two, because that is the earth's conscious level at the present time.

So, my cosmic guides tell me that there will be a profusion of these signs in your crop fields from now on.

In meditation, using the key (figures Three / Five) proceed with the three main colours, as already explained, white, pink and blue. The key fits in the centre of the wheel. Each colour from the eight points of the wheel (figures Five/Six) makes a pure white beam which can be used to heal the earth of negativity.

In the middle of the night, I was woken up with pictures that simplify this mechanism. (See figures Seven and Eight, centre pages)

On healing the land from negative to positive or on releasing trapped spirits the above figures represent the mechanism. In these figures, you will note, that this time the key is yourself.

I know of many people who have had visions of these, figures Seven and Eight, along with a building, monument, person etc.

In other words, we are being instructed to help where most needed at the right time in the right place. Please note that these figures are only rough and not detailed, purely to be used as a guide only.

Anyway, it was thanks to Alec querying the dimensions of the Celtic Cross that the similarities between the wheel was made. When I went to see the medium in Wiltshire, she saw the finished carved Celtic Cross and told me it was quite beautiful. I look forward to seeing the finished carving.

The cross has always been important to me. As a teenager, it was the only article of jewellery that I wore. I still wear a plain gold cross but now also, the Celtic Cross.

The next day Dave telephoned.

'Is it all right if I bring someone to see you. This man has a problem.' He said.

The problem was psoriasis. He had a lifetime with this problem which was now getting worse. He had also been to hospitals, specialists etc. and now was looking at alternative medicine.

Psoriasis is not curable and is hereditary. Well, could I help? As usual, I return to prayer.

Mary Magdalene was with me. I felt her energy, her vibration.

'Jane, use the stone which was at the foot of the Celtic Cross in Nevern.'

I closed my eyes and a picture was forming of all the ingredients I would need to make a cream which would help. Mary told me that I would not be alone in making this cream. Apart from the stone, there were two other ingredients in the pure cream which would have to come out after one week.

I telephoned Dave back and told him that I would be able to see him in one week's time. I also told him what happened.

That Sunday evening, I prepared the cream. Andromada was there helping. When it was prepared, Andromada told me to hold the container and close my eyes. I saw her, she is so beautiful. Andromada then asked me if it was all right if she entered me. How I love her, the feeling I cannot describe. I felt her energy, her special vibration of love flow through me and into the container.

I relaxed and placed the cream down on the table.

I opened my eyes. I now felt a new energy, one I recognised from Nevern. It was the living Christ. I felt Him come towards me and enter. That moment I cannot explain how I felt. This man must be very special to have two wonderful helpers.

Andromada told me afterwards that he must not have the cream unless he was able to pick up the energy himself. This I could prove by teaching him to dowse with the rods and the crystal.

I met him the following Sunday and found he was already on the Spiritual Pathway. He was able to dowse quite easily and healed an area on the map. One of his original sins was in Caerphilly Castle and this he had already figured out for himself. He had visited Caerphilly Castle on many occasions.

Unfortunately, he had one problem with a past life. On that occasion, he was a judge and he was still judging. My Lord has taught me never to judge others as you yourself will be judged. Each and every person is on a learning life experience. It is the way you solve your problems is the way you learn. These problems, as already discussed, are a learning package from God. Wrestle joyfully with difficulty and seek The Lord Thy God for help.

One of my son's friends is a girl, a very large tough girl. This girl had been in trouble with the police. When David had a problem with school, unfortunately, he didn't come to me but to this girl. David went to school in another district and those children also attending this school from this area, were being picked on.

Chris was worried about the company David was keeping. Unbeknown to us, this girl had not only befriended David but was looking after him. The bullies not content to stay in their own district came looking for trouble in our area. Unfortunately, they put one boy in hospital and another had thirteen stitches in his head. David was frightened to go to school or even to walk the streets to see his friends.

One day, I caught him mitching and I was so surprised as it was quite out of character. Frightened, he went back to school. He never told me the truth. He never came home that night. We were worried sick. Chris had seen him earlier with a skinhead and this girl and had decided he was in bad company. When he tried to get hold of him he ran. Poor kid, he really was badly scared and knew he was in trouble with his dad.

My guides told me he was all right and the following day showed me where he was. It transpired, that knowing the children had been beaten up, this girl not only was protecting them but also giving food and shelter. The skinhead Chris had seen David with was the boy with the thirteen stitches in his head. You guessed it, he had to shave his hair off due to his injuries. So do not judge, everything is for a reason as Chris found out this time.

I thanked this girl for looking after my son and thank goodness, the situation has now been sorted out. Two of the bullies have been expelled from school and the third is in prison for grievous bodily harm.

I also learned a lesson from that experience. I was worried sick about David and couldn't sleep. All of a sudden voices started, persecution. I hadn't experienced that since first becoming a medium. I knew I was being attacked by the lower levels, the negative levels, because they could.

I returned to prayer and to My God. It didn't take long this time to rise above it. All my unseen friends were helping and sending strength for me to regain control. I fell asleep in the afternoon when it was all over. I felt euphoria as energy surged into me from my heavenly guides.

Afterwards, I did the cards.

The cards told me that I had mastered and overcome the negative/dark forces which attacked me when I was at my lowest ebb. By seeking God, angels had been sent to help and guide. Do not deny their help, all you have to do is to ask.

CHAPTER ELEVEN

The Aquarian Age

I have had many guides and I know I can call on them when I need them. The medium in Wiltshire was right, I now have the company of another Thunder Being, a Cosmic Light, her name is Atlanta. Atlanta, I now know is a water creature. Her terrain are the ocean's depths. When I first met her, in meditation, I was surprised as she doesn't walk but glide. She wears very little except a blue wrap around with straps at the top. Her long, wavy hair is honey coloured and most people would think she looked like a mermaid but I have never seen fins or a tail.

I woke up early one morning, around 4.00 AM, for one brief second I was in water surrounded by many types of colourful fish. Wherever I looked there were fish, so many fish, all different types, colours, sizes etc. I knew I was with Atlanta then, as I am now.

As you can guess from her name she is a spirit of Atlantis. She is with me today as she wishes to let us know that the Aquarian Age is very much like it's sign, the water age.

No one is certain about the exact time of change but it will come. God Has decided, in His Infinite Wisdom, to allow this planet survival without any further intervention. We will be on our own in the future. In other words, all the positive and negative physical guides from other worlds must depart by a certain date. We will not be entirely alone. The sixty four teachers are here to help the change.

The changes are already happening around you. Atlanta tells me that I am half way through my learning process. All that I learn, I will teach, talk and write. I know now that I have another two, possibly three, years of learning.

The Aquarian Age does not have to be doom and gloom as everybody seems to think it will be. Possible earthquakes and disasters, even the drawing of large comets to our earth due to negativity. These all can be avoided. On healing the earth I noticed that it regularly changes back negative, it is an ongoing process. It just proves to me how negative the people are.

I have a channelled message direct from the Council. The wisdom of this message is simple and if people pay attention then the outcome could be very different.

'At the beginning there was heaven and hell, but God saw that this was not a way for lost souls to learn the way to righteousness. The path is left now to the individual soul groups gathered together by the Will of God. Angels watch over these soul groups bringing divine messages of the way forward and the way to put things right, which were done wrong. The devil also has a hand in these soul groups by stopping the divine messages coming through which leads to misinterpretation.

To help eradicate the problem, God makes sure his pupils understand that the crown is 'The Crown of God' anything other than the crown messages must be deemed as wrongful thought.

The devil has for centuries tried to resume what he sees as his rightful place amongst the High Council. However, God had dictated that those who hear the devil and obey his commandments have a means to resume their rightful path. Each soul group has a teacher who will know this knowledge and help the others to overcome wrongful messages.

Seek The Lord, Your Master and He will help you to salvation away from the devil. Your Lord will come to you when you ask, to strengthen you and give you courage to overcome negative thoughts. God's way is gentle, loving, you will know the difference when chaos enters your body. God is love, love is the way. When something is done without love it creates thought which is negative which gives wings to the devil. Careful, every thought, word and deed is important at this very precarious time.

God's energy is powerful and brought to you with love. In high energy, every thought pattern, word pattern and deed can become. If you imagine the devil as powerful, he will be to you. If you imagine the devil as a sorrowful soul, without meaning, then he will be.

Your very thoughts can give wing to flight. If you imagine the world as a beautiful place in high meditation with God's energy, it will be to you.

Not only can we eradicate negativity from this world, we can create a world of our own choosing. Mother Earth has chosen survival. To help her every negative soul will have a positive guide/soul teacher. The physical might not or may be aware of this guide.'

There is much more but that will come later in the chapter as I wish to explain a few things.

The dominant world governments know of this knowledge as they have been in contact with the dark/negative sides for some time. Although, in their defence, I don't think they were aware of it to start with. With advancing technology, the governments have sought help with various earth problems in a way, to them, which was positive. Unfortunately, the lights have not been altogether successful in bringing forward the alternative way.

However, nothing is wrong and nothing is right, it is all a learning experience. The people in the governments that now hold the power on this earth are leaning too, as well as those dark/negative cosmic helpers.

To maintain control, people like myself who wish to get the knowledge out have been persecuted and ridiculed. The time has come for all to realise things are not going to stay the same in the near future.

The Aquarian Age is to start in 1999 with the dawning of a new learning experience. Through this world learning experience will come peace. As this book has shown, through life's learning experiences knowledge is gained by the individual. We are about to experience a world learning package direct from God. The Aquarian Age is one of change, but it doesn't have to be for the worse.

Atlanta is teaching me the knowledge that was lost all those centuries ago in Atlantis. The Aquarian Age is the beginning of a way of life which will eradicate sinful thought, word and deed. Some are already learning and seeing for themselves that path. The Atlantians were able to communicate with their higher soul consciously in order to progress and act positively in life and to each other.

The knowledge of the healing processes are already being taught. The tunnels that I saw are a way of travelling through time, space and dimensions. These will become more apparent towards the end of the century. The energy will become a new source of power along with new inventions which can be used in conjunction with that energy. Some free energy devices have already been invented.

Remember, we are all lights. We all have a physical body and a higher soul body, which is light, our spirit.

It is Sunday morning and I am woken up at 6.30 AM in the morning to carry on with this last chapter. In the bedroom, there are many dimensional tunnels. This must be important. I am told that the book will be finished today. Mary Magdalene wishes also to write a message.

'All through the centuries, countless world tragedies have occurred for a reason. This reason, will soon become apparent. This time is very special and those world tragedies were a build up to a world learning experience. Each and every soul chooses to experience every life situation, whether physical or spiritual.

For example. One spirit wished to experience, during a physical lifetime, the sensation of drowning. In order to help her twin soul, her then physical husband, the drowning was to take place after the birth of their child. The husband left alone with the child was also on a learning pattern. The husband had chosen to experience bringing up children on this own and going through the tragedy of bereavement.

The way you go through the experience helps your soul to learn. On going through the experience of bereavement, the husband is then able to help others who will go through a similar situation in the future.

When a disaster has taken place, such as a plane crash or earthquake, people are too quick to think God is not there. Remember, the souls of those people caught up in those disasters have chosen to experience that life threatening situation. How can a teacher not help and understand if they have not been in that situation before.

Knowledge of these situations and experiences are not lost in a physical lifetime. Strength comes from within. How is it possible that you can help someone and have the knowledge of what to do, when the situation you have never experienced in that physical lifetime. How many times have you thought, I've done this before. But how could you know as consciously you are definite, you have never been through that experience, but sub-consciously you have.

Your spirit has been through that experience in another lifetime and you are drawing, sub-consciously, from that memory.

Memory is the next step. Memory of past lives. Memory of what you have done wrong. Memory of people and places you have known before.

God's energy has been sent, as explained. This energy will help you to remember who you are. The energy is the waking up of the subconscious. The spiritual teachers are already awake and have been eradicating and balancing their karma, going through a spiritual process of enlightenment.

Their enlightenment has taken place and they have woken up early in order to teach and guide you through yours. This is a very special time and you are all very special if you are reading this. The time of the second coming is close.'

Mary has left and wow what a message. I am told I can have a break now. I have just been told who is the next messenger. I am very honoured. It will be My Master. Mary Magdalene and My Master are usually together.

'In the Bible it states that there is a chosen group. Heaven will be made available to all. No one group is special. All are special, all of you. As Mary has stated, each and every soul is on a learning experience. On enlightenment, your reward is heaven. All the gifts that Jane has been given, you can have. God's energy is not for a chosen group but for everybody.

Each and every spirit chosen to experience this very special time in earth's history is honoured. It has not been easy. Each and every one of you is honoured and favoured amongst the other worlds. Yes, there are other worlds and yes, they too are part of you. Instead of selfish thoughts, remember, that we are all one of the same. If you hurt another, you hurt yourself.

The time has come for change, a new way of life. A new way of thinking. This world, will again, be a beautiful place full of God's love. In my special places you will find me. I will be there for all of you. Remember, you only have to ask. One of those special places is in your heart. Listen to your sub-conscious voice, your inner voice, which helps and guides. Remember, we are all part of the same God. God's energy is contained in every living thing, including the other worlds. They too, are a part of God. We are all His children.'

The High Council consists of many spiritual leaders of the other worlds. My Lord is a member of that High Council along with Merlin and Mendassa. Each and every member helps all of the planets when they need it most. As I have previously mentioned, there is a spiritual battle going on at this very moment.

I have up until writing this book, in meditation, put the three main crystal colours on the earth; white for spirituality; pink of love and blue of healing. We all have free will and can choose our pathway.

Unfortunately, with the energy on this earth being so negative it has not been easy. You really are a horrible, violent lot. All that violence and negativity I have channelled through this mediation. I am definitely a changed person.

The channelling has sometimes been horrendous. The foul imagination of the devil I have experienced. You occult worshippers do not realise what you are doing. You are playing with something you do not understand. All that you have created I have seen and got rid of. I sometimes get very much affected by this negativity and it is only through my faith in God that I have come through such bitter battles.

Yes, it does affect me and Yes I do feel it. Our minds, your minds are like sewers. Merlin is right. The devil is a very real entity, he does exist. His greatest achievement is making us believe that he doesn't exist. He has ruled this planet for far too long.

Return to your faith and become enlightened to a better way of life. I am sorry, I am a little bitter about that part of my experiences. It has only been through my faith, that I have succeeded in getting rid of some of the planet's negativity and for that I have been attacked by the devil on numerous occasions.

All the persecution I have suffered by the dark/negative forces had made me determined to see God's Plan through. I am not special, I am weak, but my faith has been tested over and over again. The devil has tempted me, tried to corrupt me and has fed false information to me and others around me. I now know the difference and that battle I face on a daily basis.

The persecution I face is for writing this book. This book can be used like an instruction manual with examples to help guide you.

The devil can be overcome, but only through faith, strong faith. Do not worry too much, the spiritual teachers are judged and attacked more harshly than the students.

Merlin is back with me and I feel a lot better. Forgive that last page, it had to be said.

Merlin has shown me a way in which I can use materials that have been made with spirit's help. One day, he asked me to get a very special container. It was a glass bottle and as soon as I picked it up I knew it was different. This bottle is green with a cherub sitting on the front. The cherub is made from metal which is stuck on the front of the bottle. I bought it. With my heavenly guides, I was directed to certain ingredients to make a very special liquid. The glass bottle was part of the process. Whosoever made or designed this bottle left their vibration.

Along with My Master, The Living Christ and Andromada, further vibrations and energy were focused into that glass bottle and liquid contained therein. I do not know, as yet, who this is for. All I can say is that they are honoured.

However, Merlin showed me that with the crystal I use for dowsing, I could distinguish what material has a special vibration from spirit. If the crystal goes clockwise, then it is manufactured without spirit help - for materialism/negative. If the crystal goes anti-clockwise, the substance or article made is made with the help of spirit.

For spirit to help a physical person to make something they must have faith. In helping to make an article, they leave behind a code in vibration. These vibrations, in conjunction with other vibrations or energy can be used to make something quite different. I feel that my next job will be making a note of all those different vibrations and what they can do. These vibrations are almost musical, each has a note and combined with other notes can change.

I am being driven by Merlin to research Quantum Physics and the knowledge he brings me is very radical for today. I started on this path not realising where it would take me, but I do know, that it is not over yet.

I have asked Merlin to be with others, so they could learn. He does this begrudgingly, as I found out. One girl told me that Merlin was with her to help, I had asked him, as

she so badly needed good directional help and guidance. I told her that she would always know when Merlin was around, he would probably give her a kiss, she would feel a tingling on her lips.

'No,' she said. 'He will not kiss me. He told me that was only for you and you alone.'

When I asked Merlin why, he told me. I am Merlin's daughter. In a previous physical lifetime I was actually Merlin's daughter. Merlin told me that on many physical lifetimes since he has taught me. Now I know why he is so special to me.

Andromada is also special to me, she is so beautiful. I had another shock coming. Apparently, we can choose whether to be male or female in a physical lifetime. How can we understand the other gender if we have not already experienced it. There again, on that subject we never learn.

Andromada had asked to be with me as in a previous lifetime we were husband and wife. I was the husband!! Again, Atlanta I had also married. Wow! now I am a bigamist. Not only a bigamist, but I also have three Sirian husbands! So we all experience every learning pattern imaginable.

That comes nicely on to my next subject, which is imagination. As a child, my parents told me I had a vivid imagination. I would relate stories at quite a young age. These stories did not come out of any nursery book.

Imagination is another part of it. This is our spirit's way in helping us to regain memory. Not all of imagination is fact. Inside the story is a sprinkling of truth. Listen to your children. Their innocence make them very vulnerable to spirit suggestion. They can usually see and hear spirit at a young age. We tell our children to grow up and stop imagining things. Their imaginary friends to not exist to us, but they do to them. In my son's bedroom is a wonderful vibration. I know that vibration, it is love. He is being visited by his Grandparents.

We lose this ability quite quickly, as in growing up our innocence disappears. We are literally told that, it is all in our imagination. How can we be so cruel. The imagination is everything. In it is a sprinkling of truth.

My husband tells me that I view the world through rose coloured glasses. He is right. The world is a beautiful place, full of beautiful people. Imagine it and it will come true for you. My Lord has always taught us to remain like children, innocent with love in our hearts for ourselves and for others.

In returning to our faith it is easier for the spirit guides to help. I am never alone. Sometimes I am lonely but never alone.

I was told recently that I would leave my present job and have time off to write this book. I was not looking for a job and had no intention of leaving my present position. I was told that in October of this year it would happen.

Well, it did. I was asked by a previous colleague in a different firm if I would like to join them.

I thought about it and was very undecided. During those days, guess what, Hilary was working just across the way. Although she is seeking a career in acting, at this time she was temping.

We went to lunch on the Monday and I handed in my notice that very afternoon. Thank you Hilary for helping me at that time. We all have free will and my spirit guides were leaving it to me.

I left the same day. As I was going to work for a competitor I was put on gardening leave for a month. My guides are never wrong.

Oh! remember that book, the one in Castle Morgraig. Well, I've just written it. Merlin told me, at the time, that the book would come out in September of this year. It did, I started to write in September.

At this stage, I would like to thank all my wonderful guides, who have been there for me when I needed them most. Also a big thank you to Hilary for proof reading this book. Remember, all you have to do is to ask. I will finish this book with one of Ali's poems, it is so beautiful.

Dreamscape

Have you ever flown within a dream-
to distant lands you have never seen?
Have you closed your eyes and taken flight-
to a far away fantasy in the darkness of night?
And as you awake from your sleep-
do you remember dreams you long to keep?
Never forget how to use your wings-
because coming back is one of the hardest things.

God Bless, Jane

SPIRITUAL PROTECTION

I always commence spiritual protection with the following prayers:-

Lord's Prayer

Our Father which art in heaven, Hallowed be thy Name. Thy kingdom come. Thy will be done in earth, As it is in heaven. Give us this day our daily bread. And forgive us our trepasses, As we forgive them that treespass against us. And lead us not into temptation; But deliver us from evil: For thine is the kingdom, The power, and the glory, For ever and ever. Amen.

The Creed

I Believe in one God the Father Almighty, Maker of heaven and earth, And of all things visible and invisible:

And in one Lord Jesus Christ, the only begotten Son of God, Begotten of his Father before all worlds, God of God, Light of Light, Very God of very God, Begotten, not made, Being of one substance with the Father; By whom all things are made, Who for us men, and for our salvation came down from heaven, And was incarnate by the Holy Ghost of the Virgin Mary, And was made man, And was crucified also for us under Pontius Pilate. He suffered and was buried, And the third day he rose again according to the Scriptures, And ascended into heaven, And sitteth on the right hand of the Father. And he shall come again with glory to judge both the quick and the dead: Whose kingdom shall have no end.

And I believe in the Holy Ghost, The Lord and giver of life, Who proceedeth from the Father and the Son, Who with the Father and the Son together is worshipped and glorified, Who spake by the Prophets. And I believe one Catholick and Apostolick Church. I acknowledge one Baptism for the remission of sins, And I look for the Resurrection of the dead, And the life of the world to come. Amen.

Bring the pure white light in through the feet, through the body and out through the top of your head. Surround yourself in this white light, this pure white energy and if there are any muddy spots, flick them out like a brilliant white firework. Then bring in the blue of healing and the pink of love.

Bring down a golden pyramid of protection, over and under you and fill it with the pure white light. If you have headaches or depression and you know you are being attacked by the dark/negative forces places mirrors on the outside of the pyramids which, in effect, will rebound any negativity back to the source attacking.

The best form of spiritual protection is to ask Our Father for help and courage to overcome the dark/negative forces. Faith is the main form of spiritual protection.

PYRAMID PROTECTION

If you imagine a pyramid over and under you, then twist it so that the two pyramids form the eight points at the centre where you stand (See figures 9 & 10). This, in effect, is the meditation wheel/celtic cross. A simple way to understand this procedure is to have two small pyramids. If you place one on top of the other - you have a diamond shape. If you twist the sides until there are eight even points you have the wheel/celtic cross.

SPIRITUAL HEALING

The same form as spititual protection except when healing use the following prayer after bringing in the three colours; pink, blue and white.

'Dear Father, with your beautiful white light, heal the leys, heal the energy. Spirits trapped go towards the white light, do not be afraid you will be with your family, friends and loved ones. Amen.'

To heal a photograph of a person or map of an area use the orange light. After saying the above prayer push the orange light through the palm shakra until the photograph/map becomes warm.

To heal a person push the blue, pink and white through their palm shakras from your own.

Once again, what is in your heart is more important. Faith is the best form of spiritual healing.